DEFI 2023 INVESTING

A GUIDE FOR FUTURE OPPORTUNITIES FOR
INVESTMENT IN A VOLATILE MARKET;
DEFYING THE ODDS: WHY DEFI IS STILL WORTH
INVESTING; DEFI IS THE FUTURE OF FINANCE

NFT TRENDING CRYPTO ART

WANT FREE NEW BOOK LAUNCHES?

EMAIL US AT:
mindsetmastership@gmail.com

SCAN ME FOR A BONUS

https://bonus.mindsetmastership.com/defi-2023-investing

ARE YOU READY TO JOIN IN ON THE NEW CRYPTO REVOLUTION?

Introducing *Investing in Metaverse, NFTs, Blockchain, and DeFi: Taking Advantage Of The New Crypto Economy*

IN THIS FREE BONUS GUIDE DISCOVER:

- Metaverse - 5 Most Lucrative Projects in 2023!
- NFTs - Top 10 Trending NFT Fractionalization Projects in 2023!
- Blockchain - 5 Cryptocurrencies Under $1 Skyrocketing in 2023!
- DeFi - 6 DEXs That Will Revolutionize the Crypto Market in 2023!

PLUS BONUS NEW FREE BOOK RELEASES!

SCAN THE QR CODE TO CLAIM YOUR FREE BONUS NOW!

https://bonus.mindsetmastership.com/defi-2023-investing

JOIN OUR NFT CRYPTO ART ENTREPENUER POWER GROUP

To help reinforce the learning's from our books, I strongly suggest you join our well-informed powerhouse community on Facebook.

Here, you will connect and share with other like-minded people to support your journey and help you grow.

Follow and Like our Facebook Page
to get the latest updates on our new book releases:
https://www.facebook.com/nfttrending/

To Join Our Personal Support Group Go To:
https://www.facebook.com/groups/nfttrending/

OUR OTHER BOOKS ON AMAZON

Follow us on Amazon:
NFT Trending Crypto Art

Decentralized Finance (DeFi) Investment Guide; Platforms, Exchanges, Lending, Borrowing, Options Trading, Flash Loans & Yield-Farming: Bull & Bear of Bitcoin ... (Decentralized Finance (DeFi) Books Book 2)

Decentralized Finance DeFi 2022 Investing Guide, Lend, Trade, Save Bitcoin & Ethereum do Business in Cryptocurrency Peer to Peer (P2P) Staking, Flash Loans ... (Decentralized Finance (DeFi) Books Book 3)

NFT (Non Fungible Tokens), Guide; Buying, Selling, Trading, Investing in Crypto Collectibles Art. Create Wealth and Build Assets: Or Become a NFT Digital ... to Advanced The Ultimate Handbook Book 1)

NFT Investing for Beginners to Advanced, Make Money; Buy, Sell, Trade, Invest in Crypto Art, Create Digital Assets, Earn

Passive income in Cryptocurrency, ... to Advanced The Ultimate Handbook Book 2)

NFT (Non-Fungible Token) Investing Guide Create Your Crypto Art Marketplace Platform: Learn to, Buy, Trade, Hold, The Most Valuable Digital NFT Art Collections ... to Advanced The Ultimate Handbook Book 3)

NFT (Non Fungible Tokens) Investing Guide for Beginners to Advance 2022 & Beyond : NFTs Handbook for Artists, Real Estate & Crypto Art, Buying, Flipping ... to Advanced The Ultimate Handbook Book 4)

Blockchain Investing; Bitcoin, Cryptocurrency, NFT, DeFi, Metaverse, Smart contracts, Distributed Ledgers, DAO, Web 3.0 & 5G: The Next Technology Revolution To Change Everything Ultimate Guide

Ethereum 2.0 Cryptocurrency Investing Book: A Beginners Guide to Invest in The Eth2 Crypto Merge, The Future Internet Money Millionaire Maker

CONTENTS

INTRODUCTION

The decentralized finance (DeFi) world is constantly evolving, and for enthusiasts always looking for potential opportunities, 2023 promises to be an exciting year. In this book, we'll discuss the current state of the DeFi market and look at the trends and events likely to shape the industry over the years to come. From new protocols and platforms to innovative use cases and emerging asset classes, there is no shortage of potential opportunities to discover. With expert insights and analysis, this book provides a comprehensive guide for anyone looking to stay ahead of the curve in the fast-moving world of DeFi. Whether you are a seasoned DeFi professional or new to the space, this book is the perfect resource for staying informed and finding success in decentralized finance.

A new financial system called decentralized finance allows users to send and receive money from any other user. These peer-to-peer interactions are made possible by smart contracts. Users may trade digital assets without a centralized exchange, earn interest on their cryptocurrency holdings, lend or borrow Ether-based assets, and more.

DeFi lending platforms allow users to generate stablecoins and earn interest on cryptocurrencies. The cryptocurrency market reached record highs in 2021, but since the collapse of FTX in 2022, it has driven investors into self-custody. Almost 97% of all cryptocurrency stolen in the first three months of 2022 has been taken from DeFi protocols.

Furthermore, leading crypto lenders and exchanges failed when the market value fell. Despite the crash, the era of decentralized finance may have just begun. The DeFi market is anticipated to reach $800 billion in 2022 as more institutional investors join the sector. Regulators are in a bind between being too rigid or too tolerant with this emerging new order.

Scaling and other cutting-edge strategies are being developed to lower transaction costs, which is why decentralized finance appeals to financial organizations due to the interest it generates from investors. Although, there are still many issues that need to be resolved first, such as regulation and transparency. Some are promoting DeFi as the ultimate financial future solution that may eliminate regulatory malfeasance. DeFi aims to undermine traditional financial middlemen (banks, brokers, wealth managers, etc.).

Cryptocurrency and decentralized infrastructure are concepts considered different since DeFi provides different financial instruments with a traditional bank or exchange requirement. Moreover, this book will explore the probable top DeFi stocks to watch in 2023.

DeFi is now a $100 billion market, starting from a $1 billion industry in 2019. Blockchain-based financial services will have to overcome practical and financial obstacles to compete.

This book will provide tremendous upside potential for those willing to venture into this exciting space, making them worthwhile investments for those serious about growing their wealth through rapidly evolving crypto economies!

Read *on to learn* more...

Dear Reader,

As independent authors, it's often difficult to gather reviews compared with much bigger publishers.

Therefore, please leave a review on the platform where you bought this book.

KINDLE:

LEAVE A REVIEW HERE < click here >

Many thanks,

Author Team

1

DECENTRALIZED FINANCE (DEFI)

A rising number of people are turning to decentralized finance to access banking alternatives. Decentralized financial services and the widespread adoption of blockchain technology have given rise to a new universe dubbed "Decentralized Finance" (DeFi). Access to financial services is not an issue wherever dealings are protected, costs are kept to a minimum, and the most recent developments in DeFi are the norm.

Several benefits are possible with decentralized finance, but the hazards must be understood first. Consequently, this book on decentralized finance development for businesses will take you through the basics of decentralized finance: what it is, how it works, and some of the essential barriers you need to know before getting started. Without further ado, let's begin.

What is Decentralized Finance (DeFi)?

A decentralized finance system, or DeFi, is based on open blockchains. The building blocks of open finance are blockchain-based smart contracts, digital assets, dApps (decentralized applications), and protocols.

Although many of us are familiar with the Bitcoin and Ethereum cryptocurrencies, only a few know that they are open-source, enormous networks that allow users to create programs that enable financial activity to flourish without the involvement of centralized organizations.

Decentralized finance has opened up a wide range of new opportunities for users to interact with the Ethereum blockchain in ways that weren't conceivable before. Using DeFi, users may trade digital assets without a centralized exchange, earn interest on their cryptocurrency holdings, lend or borrow Ethereum-based assets, and much more.

Decentralized finance is intended to offer customers an alternative to established financial institutions, which are frequently opaque and inaccessible. DeFi would contribute to a more inclusive financial system that benefits everyone by making financial services more approachable and user-friendly.

How Does DeFi Work?

As a form of decentralized finance, blockchain technology, which cryptocurrencies use, has found a home in the banking sector. The term "blockchain" describes a specific decentralized and encrypted digital ledger. Each transaction is stored in a "block" on the blockchain, which other users can verify. If every validator agrees on a transaction, the block is sealed and encrypted, and the data from the previous block is included in the new block.

The term "blockchain" refers to how the blocks are "chained" together by the data in each succeeding block. There is no way to edit a blockchain since changes to the information in earlier blocks always impact later blocks. This idea, coupled with other security measures, gives a blockchain its security.

Without the use of centralized intermediaries, decentralized finance offers a means of gaining access to financial services. For instance, on the Ethereum blockchain, peer-to-peer interactions are made possible by smart contracts. A financial system's ability to function efficiently depends upon two key elements: the infrastructure and the currency required for operation.

Infrastructure: The DeFi platform Ethereum is used to create decentralized programs. With the help of Ethereum, you may build smart contracts that specify a set of guidelines that must meet requirements before a contract can be signed. Remember, a smart contract cannot be changed once it has been implemented.

Currency: A coin that can communicate with the various protocols is required to build a safe, dependable decentralized finance system. DeFi often employs the DAI stablecoin as its medium of exchange, and a decentralized stablecoin tied to the US Dollar is called DAI.

Now that we know what DeFi is and how it operates let's compare DeFi to the established financial system.

Centralized Finance (CeFi) and Traditional Finance (TradFi)

Different from traditional, centralized banking and financial institutions is decentralized finance.

Centralized finance: The funds in centralized finance are kept by banks and other third parties, who also help with the transfer of funds between parties; each party levies a fee for the use of its services. The card details are obtained from the merchant and sent to the credit card network by an acquiring bank to complete the transaction.

The network approves the charge and requests payment from the bank. Each link in the chain is compensated for its services because retailers typically have to pay for credit and debit cards. All financial operations, such as loan applications and local bank services, are under the control of centralized finance.

Fact: DeFi's goals include lowering transaction times and boosting financial service accessibility.

Traditional finance: There are some inherent decentralized differences to consider in order to differentiate between Decentralized Finance and Traditional Finance, even though Decentralized Finance is merely an advanced version of the finance structure with the same core working in receiving and giving money. So let's learn about the distinctions.

1. Institutions and workers are not in charge of DeFi's operations. In the DeFi context, their function is carried out through algorithms implemented as smart contracts or by coding. DeFi apps operate automatically after a smart contract is posted to the blockchain, unlike traditional finance, where intermediaries like banks manage financial processes.

2. The fact that DeFi offers the capability of code transparency is one of the standout DeFi features that amply demonstrate the distinctions between DeFi and conventional banking apps. This makes it easy for anybody to audit, which fosters user trust because everyone has the chance to comprehend the operation of the contract. Additionally, privacy concerns are never raised because the transactions are anonymous. Security flaws could occur in traditional finance since intermediaries control the monetary processes.

3. The DeFi ecosystem uses dApps development, a different kind of blockchain application intended to operate internationally right out of the box. No matter the region of the world you are in, you can access DeFi networks and services as opposed to the traditional financial system, which limits financial institutions' services to their local areas. For example, you can only open a bank account in the nation where the bank is located.

4. Anyone can develop and use decentralized finance applications. Unlike traditional finance, there are no accounts or gatekeepers on this front, and consumers communicate with smart contracts straight from DeFi cryptocurrency wallets.

5. Similar to Lego, the new decentralized finance apps are constructed and assembled by combining different DeFi products. For instance, combining decentralized exchanges, stablecoins, and prediction markets can create new businesses. However, in the conventional financial system, each application is made specifically for a given task with a particular purpose.

Why Use DeFi?

One of the central tenets of DeFi is the use of peer-to-peer (P2P) financial transactions. When two parties agree to exchange cryptocurrencies for goods or services without the involvement of a third party, this is known as a P2P DeFi transaction.

In DeFi, peer-to-peer lending can satisfy a person's desire for a loan. An algorithm would connect peers who concurred with the lender's terms and then grant a loan. Through a decentralized application or dApp, P2P payments are made and proceed like blockchain transactions. Using DeFi enables:

- **Accessibility:** A DeFi platform is accessible to anybody with an internet connection, and transactions can take place anywhere in the world.
- **Low transaction costs and high-interest rates:** Using DeFi networks, two parties can directly negotiate interest rates and make loans.
- **Security and transparency:** Smart contracts recorded on a blockchain are open for everyone to study, and records of transactions performed are also available, but they do not identify your name. Because blockchains are immutable, they cannot be altered.
- **Autonomy:** DeFi platforms are independent of any centralized financial institutions, making them impervious to failure or misfortune. DeFi protocols' decentralized structure significantly reduces this risk.
- **Fast Fact:** DeFi peer-to-peer lending does not eliminate the possibility of interest and other costs. The lender can be located worldwide, so you will have many more options.

How can DeFi be Used?

Before utilizing DeFi, there are a few things to be aware of.

Get the wallet

You will require an Ethereum-compatible digital wallet to use DeFi. Users can safely store thousands of NFTs and cryptocurrencies in their wallets.

Purchase relevant DeFi cryptocurrency

It would help if you bought a decentralized finance cryptocurrency asset native to the Ethereum blockchain, such as Ether, to communicate with DeFi. Determine which alternative is most suitable for you in light of your comfort level with risk and your desired return on investment.

Your wallet must be connected to the decentralized exchange.

If you've got some bitcoin for decentralized finance and a digital wallet, you're ready to start trading on a decentralized exchange. You may start using decentralized finance to trade cryptocurrencies and have access to lending and borrowing services by following these easy steps.

How to put money into DeFi?

DeFi investments can be made in a variety of ways. The easiest way to expose you to DeFi, in general, is to purchase Ether or another coin that uses DeFi. Buying a coin with DeFi power exposes you to almost the entire DeFi market.

You can deposit cryptocurrencies with a DeFi lending facility to earn income on your holdings. You can obtain greater interest rates if you are willing to deposit money for longer. The interest rate you receive on your deposit may be either fixed or variable and subject to market fluctuations.

Since there is a significant demand for deposits across the several DeFi platforms, a "yield farming" business has developed. Yield farmers regularly track the current interest rates and incentives provided by other platforms and deposit money on whichever platform offers the highest interest rate or another incentive.

The yield farmers optimize their income by shifting their deposits to the alternative platform if it starts to offer a better incentive. Yield farmers continue migrating their money from platform to platform as incentives continuously change.

If you wish to influence the future of DeFi protocols, you can invest in Uniswap's UNI coin (CRYPTO:UNI). As a governance token, UNI offers you voting power over the direction of the Uniswap protocol in proportion to your ownership. The future of the service attracts more user interest due to their participation in the decision-making process, and larger holdings of UNI are needed to maintain significant decision-making ability. The token's price may rise sharply as a result of this dynamic.

How is DeFi Applicable in the Real World?

The widespread use of DeFi systems and methods has the potential to significantly improve a lot of the world's 2.5 billion unbanked citizens. This section will cover some of the most significant applications of DeFi. So, let's get going!

Lowering expenses: The remittance sector, where international workers send billions of dollars to their families across borders, has excessive fees. The trends in decentralized finance services may allow for a more than 50% reduction of these costs. This encourages economic growth while increasing worker productivity.

Borrowing and lending: The other challenging area that can be managed by concentrating on DeFi's advantages is loans. It is currently difficult for the unbanked to obtain credit because of a low credit score or a complicated banking history. Credit checks are unnecessary, thanks to the DeFi platforms' ability to link borrowers and lenders.

Asset financing: Stablecoins, tokenized Bitcoin, lending and borrowing platforms, and other integrated DeFi financial instruments have all been made possible by the DeFi ecosystem. By implementing immutable smart contracts on Ethereum, DeFi developers have unlocked numerous new asset-decentralized finance and risk management potential.

DeFi protocols, using flash loans finalized in a single transaction and collateralized loans with DeFi money or digital assets have developed novel ways to obtain liquidity without relying on centralized exchanges.

Supply chain administration: Decentralized technology based on the Ethereum blockchain has enabled peer-to-peer funding, or Decentralized Financial Infrastructure, to replace traditional, centralized financial institutions. Due to the interaction between this paradigm-shifting trend and the supply chain management industry, a variety of new prospects for reducing inefficiencies and paths for greater collaboration and decentralized financing are opening up.

A real-world example is the creation of TradeLens by Maersk and IBM. The technology makes it possible to send and retrieve documents instantly, thereby accelerating the supply chain.

These are a few illustrations of how blockchain influences the fintech industry. Blockchain is merely getting ready to design innovative use cases of DeFi platforms by eliminating errors and introducing transparency.

DeFi-Related Challenges

Each high-return financial instrument has a risk associated with it. There will almost undoubtedly be a list of difficulties for DeFi as well.

Utilizing cryptocurrency tools safely and effectively requires specific knowledge and associated risk. Users now must protect their important possessions and adhere to multi-factor authentication with the utmost discretion.

Many security-related issues have also occurred, necessitating the introduction of strict security and privacy algorithms by different decentralized financial development organizations. While the solution designers have taken up the responsibility, DeFi users should also be informed of any modifications to the terms of service for various wallets, exchanges, DeFi protocols, DeFi platforms, and other DeFi crypto initiatives.

Additionally, before making any investment decisions, investors can review historical data and benchmarks in the case of traditional currencies. However, DeFi users enjoy a different privilege. It is challenging to evaluate the associated risk, given the absence of historical data. The users must then conduct considerable independent research as a result of this.

Well-known DeFi projects

MakerDAO: the decentralized reserve bank is a stablecoin initiative in which each stablecoin is backed by cryptocurrency as collateral and pegged to the US dollar. On the Maker Oasis dApp platform, business owners can also create their own DAI stablecoin. Maker aims to provide the solution to how DeFi can become a reserve bank and as such is much more than a stablecoin initiative. Consider how the Federal Open Market Committee of the Federal Reserve votes on the Fed Funds rate, holders of MKR can even cast votes on important decisions like stability fees.

Compound: Lending and borrowing

It is a loan and borrowing dApp enabled by blockchain, one of the most thriving subsectors of open finance. Users can use their cryptocurrency as collateral in the compound contract and borrow money using it. Then it dynamically adjusts the interest rate based on supply and demand, open lending procedures, and automatic matching of lenders and borrowers.

Uniswap: token exchange

This DeFi cryptocurrency exchange platform allows users to trade well-known tokens directly from their wallets and is powered by smart contracts. It uses a distinct process known as Automated Market Making to settle deals close to market price. Users can also become liquidity providers by providing the cryptocurrency to the Uniswap contract and earning a cut of the exchange feed.

Augur: market prediction platform

This is a product for decentralized prediction markets, where users can cast votes on the results of events and give their votes a value. Despite being relatively new, prediction market platforms take a futuristic look by allowing users to foresee the future by drawing on the collective wisdom of the masses.

PoolTogether: zero loss savings platform

Participants can deposit DAI stablecoins into a pool on the platform. One person wins all the interest at the end of each month, and everyone else receives their initial investment back.

Finance will be decentralized in the future

The industry has been around since the beginning of human history, and cryptocurrencies are just the most recent digital product to emerge from it. The DeFi and open finance ecosystem is expected to mirror every fiat-based financial service we use today eventually.

The primary safety mechanism for the first generation of DeFi apps is using collateral. To borrow more DeFi cryptocurrency, you must first acquire a DeFi platform coin and then put it up as collateral. Recent updates to DeFi apps have sparked a wave of disruption in the insurance industry. Too much collateral is put up for many current DeFi loans (the loans are rendered fundamentally safe by the significant asset cushion held in reserve).

In addition, DeFi crypto wallets have become the focal point of all digital asset transactions. You can think of it like a dashboard, as it shows you the assets you own and the proportion of those assets tied to particular open finance protocols like pools, loans, and insurance policies.

We are also noticing a trend toward more distributed forms of leadership and decision-making. DeFi projects include master keys that allow DeFi platform development solution providers to shut down dApps to simplify upgrades or protect instances of bad code, despite the current emphasis on the phrase "decentralized" in DeFi. On the other hand, members of the DeFi community are actively looking for methods to implement voting mechanisms for stakeholder decisions, which would greatly expand the potential applications of DeFi.

Something new is happening on the front of the open financial system after all the speculating and POCs about new DeFi possibilities are being planned and made: cryptocurrencies are bringing money online and offering people ways to generate money on dApps. Each new disruptive product introduction challenges our ideas about how money works.

We observers find it fascinating that the future of decentralized finance and money is in the hands of anyone who can code.

Clarifying DeFi

Decentralized finance, or DeFi, has the potential to upend the financial sector. Note that it is similar to but distinct from cryptocurrencies like Bitcoin (CRYPTO:BTC). The Ethereum (CRYPTO:ETH) blockchain and all the coins based on it are especially linked to DeFi.

DeFi technology generates decentralized money and does away with the need for central banks under the power of the government to produce and manage the currency. But DeFi technology also offers a wide range of additional blockchain-based financial services applications. DeFi technology is used by fintech businesses to provide insurance, stock trading, savings accounts, and loans, among other services.

A few of the most widely used DeFi applications:

Stablecoins

The development of stablecoins, sometimes known as cryptocurrencies with stable values, was one of the initial uses of DeFi. Stablecoins are seen as excellent for making routine purchases because they are significantly less volatile than other cryptocurrencies.

DAI is an illustration of a stablecoin (CRYPTO:DAI). The coin is issued by MakerDAO, an open-source project on the Ethereum network, and is tied to the US dollar. Ether, the native token of Ethereum, serves as collateral. Ether intentionally overcollateralizes DAI, allowing the value of DAI to be steady despite changes in Ether's value.

Another stablecoin is USDC (CRYPTO:USDC), but unlike DAI, its collateral is centralized. The reserve of US dollars used to back USDC stablecoins is kept in an audited bank account.

Decentralized exchanges

Despite the decentralized nature of cryptocurrencies, several exchanges, like Coinbase (NASDAQ:COIN), serve as centralized platforms to link buyers and sellers of cryptocurrencies. Smart contracts are used by decentralized exchanges (DEXs), such as MDEX, to carry out the functions of centralized exchanges. The smart contracts provide pricing for each counterparty at or near the going market rate. By using a DEX, both parties can keep complete control over their bitcoin holdings instead of storing them in a wallet managed by a centralized exchange that might be subject to hacking.

In some marketplaces, DEX users that supply bitcoin to create liquidity might profit by sharing the transaction costs.

Prediction markets

People can wager on the results of specific events thanks to prediction markets. By altering bet structures, DeFi prediction markets afford customers higher odds of success. The accompanying costs are also reduced, and participants can wager an unlimited amount on anything. Prediction markets are significantly more difficult for centralized authorities to take down than traditional bookies.

Beyond facilitating more access to gambling, DeFi prediction markets might be helpful. Stock market forecasts that consider the size of the underlying bets are frequently reasonably accurate.

Lending and borrowing

Borrowing and lending services, among the most convenient features made possible by DeFi, are accessible to bitcoin users. Those with significant cryptocurrency holdings who desire access to liquidity in other currencies might borrow money by pledging their cryptocurrency holdings as security. Individuals can profit from increases in the value of their cryptocurrency holdings without triggering taxable events by lending their deposits to earn interest from borrowers. The decentralized application programs that enable this decentralized borrowing and lending offer interest rates that automatically fluctuate in response to changes in the cryptocurrency's supply and demand.

Is DeFi safe?

Because DeFi technology is so young, unpleasant effects occasionally happen. DeFi technology-based startups may fail (startup failure is highly prevalent), and programming mistakes can lead to lucrative possibilities for hackers. If a DeFi project you invested in or stored money with fails, you could lose all of your money.

Deposits in FDIC-insured banks are guaranteed, while there is usually no recourse for recouping lost funds on DeFi platforms. Consumers can report to the Consumer Financial Protection Bureau (CFPB) if a typical financial transaction goes wrong. Still, they have no remedy if they fall victim to a fraudulent DeFi transaction.

It's interesting to note that a different kind of DeFi program is becoming accessible to overcome these shortcomings. Those looking to safeguard themselves against losses from other smart contracts are offered decentralized insurance produced by individuals pooling their money as collateral. The premiums paid by those who are insured are collected by the individuals who contribute to the bitcoin pools.

Key features in this chapter

- Decentralized finance (DeFi), a new type of financial system, is based on securely distributed ledgers similar to those used by cryptocurrencies.
- Decentralized financial services and the widespread adoption of blockchain technology have given rise to a new universe dubbed "Decentralized Finance" (DeFi).
- A financial system's ability to function efficiently depends on two key elements: the infrastructure and the currency required for operation.
- DeFi apps operate automatically after a smart contract is posted to the blockchain, unlike traditional finance, where intermediaries like banks manage financial processes.
- Anyone can develop and use decentralized finance applications.
- By combining already existing DeFi solutions, new decentralized financial apps can be made.
- DeFi encourages a greater degree of openness and accessibility.
- People have more power over their finances thanks to decentralized financial solutions.
- The DeFi environment offers legitimate opportunities for innovation and developing DeFi services and goods.
- The widespread use of DeFi systems and methods can significantly improve many of the world's 2.5 billion unbanked citizens.

2

DEFI AND TRADFI MUST WORK TOGETHER

Decentralized and traditional finance can coexist, but only under defined standards and regulations to finance renewable energy and other urgent requirements.

The cryptocurrency market is currently experiencing a crypto winter. Bitcoin and Ethereum's Ether have lost three-quarters of their value, and numerous significant crypto lending and investment organizations have gone bankrupt.

Traditional finance or TradFi, as the crypto and DeFi (decentralized finance) movement refers to the financial and economic establishment, is also experiencing some chilly weather. The international monetary system is broken due to war, an energy and commodities crisis causing starvation and political instability, record temperatures that reveal a huge investment gap in the battle against climate change, and the greatest inflation in 40 years.

The truth is that both sides depend on one another.

DeFi and crypto must incorporate some of the regulatory and automated processes that have given TradFi functional stability if they are to be widely adopted. However, there is also a pressing need for the guardians of the world economy to investigate DeFi and crypto solutions to its numerous issues. The heavily concentrated energy sector is one area to pay attention to.

In the wake of Russia's invasion of Ukraine, talks are underway with Saudi Crown Prince Mohammed bin Salman to increase the oil supply and lower rising world prices. The definition of a centralization issue is in order to solve an economic crisis that affects all 8 billion of us, world leaders must pander to the interests of a single, unelected person.

An additional striking illustration is Germany's reliance on Russian natural gas, which limits its ability to implement sanctions against the Kremlin. Take the shutdown of the Colonial pipeline last year, caused by ransomware hackers who took advantage of the fact that 60 million people depend on the fuel it supplies. And there is one more: Hurricane Maria in 2017 left 90% of Puerto Ricans without power for months after bringing down a few high-voltage transmission lines.

As good a reason as any to support renewable energy as a solution to the climate catastrophe is vulnerability to external occurrences, which electricity system designers refer to as a lack of "redundancy." We must immediately decentralize our energy system. The solution is to recycle waste heat and energy or use renewable energy sources like solar, geothermal, and wind. They can operate on a variety of scales and are locally sourced.

But what connection exists between decentralized energy and decentralized finance? It begins with acknowledging that the world's inadequate response to our energy dilemma is not due to technological failure but a lack of money.

The Climate Policy Initiative, a think tank with headquarters in San Francisco, estimates that $632 billion was spent globally in 2019–20 on addressing climate change, significantly less than the \$4.5–\$5 trillion it claims is required yearly to achieve net zero carbon emissions by 2050.

Governments and businesses worldwide have committed to aggressive carbon reduction targets, so it is not for want of will. The problem is that there need to be more projects out there whose promised returns and influence inspire them with enough confidence.

In most cases, two components are missing: first, trustworthy, quickly actionable data with which to measure and project outcomes, and second, a source of persistent, flexible user demand that would make the production of renewable energy in locations where it is available economically viable.

The financial innovation sparked by the open-source developer communities of DeFi and crypto can solve both.

Green funding potential

The technology's ability to instantly transform data into tradable assets, resulting from its automated, nearly instantaneous peer-to-peer settlement and the power to establish distinct digital units of any size or value, offers the best chances for actionable information. The efficiencies might be huge compared to the analog world of green bonds, which requires many layers of bureaucracy and depends upon retroactive data that takes months or even years to create and verify.

With provably secure sensors and blockchain-based tracking systems, plants can instantly express that they produce green energy as one-of-a-kind, unique tokens, thanks to crypto technology. These tokens might serve as collateral for lenders in a DeFi setting. The approach offers investors remote protection by including programmable cryptocurrencies, stablecoins, or central bank digital currencies.

A massive pool of liquidity might form around these tokens as governments and ESG-compliant businesses ramp up demand for proven carbon-reducing assets, creating the deep capital markets that climate action needs.

This strategy may lower project finance costs in general. You may see the possibilities by imagining a rural Rwandan town constructing a solar microgrid using DeFi funding to run a brand-new irrigation system.

The demand issue is yet another one. Imagine that economies of scale dictate that the Rwandan microgrid must have a capacity of at least two megawatts to be financially viable, but the new irrigation system only requires 500 kilowatts. How might a low-income neighborhood with minimal electricity demands make up the difference?

It may seem contradictory to anyone who has recently joined campaigns to outlaw "wasteful" proof-of-work mining in New York and elsewhere that Bitcoin holds the solution. In contrast to other energy consumers, Bitcoin mining is not location-specific, and miners can work in almost any place. If the price is low enough to keep them profitable and competitive, they will gladly take in any community's surplus or other lost energy.

The goal should be to direct Bitcoin toward renewable sources if we can't regulate it out of existence.

What kind of energy is the cheapest? It qualifies as renewable energy. According to the Cambridge Center for Alternative Finance, the Bitcoin network already uses 53% renewable energy, not because miners are kind but profit-driven.

Given the current decline in the price of bitcoin and the likelihood that Intel's new Blockscale application-specific integrated circuits (ASICs) will result in a glut of inexpensive chips for miners, the availability of affordable energy will become a key consideration in any miner's expansion plans.

Miners will be willing and important partners for renewable energy providers if regulations don't stop them from forming relationships. They will consent to significant energy contracts that finance the construction of plants and pledge to use surplus energy output during times of low community demand to balance the grid's peaks and valleys. The economics of electricity may be made predictable and viable through mining.

Fair enough, many carbon emissions come from the remaining 47% of the Bitcoin network. According to a mid-range estimate from the Cambridge Center for Alternative Finance, the network uses 84 terawatts of electricity annually, roughly 0.38 percent of the world's total usage. The proof-of-work mechanism used by Bitcoin consumes a lot of electricity. Proof-of-stake systems, which consume far less energy, are encouraged for digital assets like non-fungible tokens.

But whether you like it or not, Bitcoin is here to stay. Mining relocates when prohibited in one location, as was the case in 2021 when a restriction in China caused a large portion of the industry to shift to the United States, Kazakhstan, and other locations.

The goal should be to drive Bitcoin toward renewable sources—or away from fossil fuel sources—if we can't regulate it out of existence. It's time for practical energy laws that eliminate support for polluting power plants and encourage Bitcoin miners to make long-term financial commitments to renewable energy suppliers with minimum capacity thresholds for local communities.

Decentralization, as well as the growth of renewable energy, are the objectives here. Let's avoid the example of El Salvador, where the government is profiting from Bitcoin mining at a government-owned geothermal plant. Instead, developing nations should support collaborations between miners and neighborhood solar microgrids to distribute wealth and increase generation capacity to achieve social objectives and grid resiliency.

Rethinking regulation

This is not to argue that there are no issues with the crypto sector. The recent financial pandemic in the industry brought to light the perils of a culture of speculation that gave rise to unchecked leverage and fraud. It is especially prevalent to exploit anonymity to front-run markets through wash trades and other pump-and-dump schemes. There needs to be more transparency and more efficient regulation.

However, given that decentralized crypto projects operate very differently from centralized financial systems, we should avoid using their antiquated regulatory frameworks. Applying a centralized approach, such as trying to hold dispersed, leaderless open-source developer groups accountable for users of the DeFi protocols they design, could increase rather than decrease dangers.

Celsius, Voyager Digital, and Three Arrows Capital were the three largest "CeFi" services that contributed to the recent financial crisis. At the same time, Terra Luna, a de facto Ponzi scam, was mere "DeFi" in the name. Real DeFi projects like Aave and Compound have so far held up exceptionally well during this rigorous stress test.

DeFi also carries some significant additional dangers. The crypto security company Immunefi calculates that hackers and breaches of smart contracts cost $670 million in the second quarter of 2022. Customers will need considerably stronger guarantees that their payments are protected if DeFi is to attract new users.

The trick is to find a balance

The management of CeFi services should be subject to greater fiduciary responsibilities from regulators; they should be treated similarly to brokerages or other regulated financial institutions. However, for DeFi activities, they should collaborate with the sector to create self-regulatory approaches that take advantage of its technological prowess and decentralized structure. Ideas include increasing the "bug bounties" that pay developers who find and correct errors, requiring recurring software audits, and regularly stress testing leverage and collateral model assumptions.

Above all, we need agreement on what decentralized systems are and if programs that aim to develop in that direction are doing so appropriately.

Before norms and standards can be formed, there must be a consensus on the frameworks and common nomenclature used by both the DeFi and TradFi communities. Although difficult, this must be completed, and more are needed.

Key features in this chapter

- It's time for practical energy laws that eliminate support for polluting power plants and encourage Bitcoin miners to make long-term financial commitments to renewable energy suppliers with minimum capacity thresholds for local communities.
- Decentralization, as well as the growth of renewable energy, are the objectives here.
- Given that decentralized crypto projects operate very differently from centralized financial systems, we should avoid using their antiquated regulatory frameworks.
- DeFi activities should work with the sector to develop self-regulatory methods that use the sector's technological skills and decentralized structure to their advantage.

Before norms and standards can be formed, there must be consensus on the frameworks and standard terminology used by both the DeFi and TradFi communities.

3

DEFI LENDING

The chances of using blockchain technology in creating financial applications have improved with the introduction of DeFi. DeFi has recently attracted a lot of interest since it has raised enormous sums of money for numerous businesses.

You might be astonished to learn that about $20.46 billion is currently secured in DeFi protocols, demonstrating the applications' significant surge in popularity. This has had an impact on the development of DeFi lending. One of the booming elements of the bitcoin ecosystem is DeFi lending. These loans enable cryptocurrency owners to lend their assets and earn high-interest rates.

DeFi lending entails providing cryptocurrency loans through a decentralized network. DeFi leads global loan growth rates for all decentralized applications. It is one of the well-known that contributors have used to lock cryptocurrency assets.

What is the Process of DeFi lending?

You are well aware that the goal of DeFi lending is to provide a permissionless, open-source, and transparent financial service environment.

Let's now address a frequently-questioned topic, "How does DeFi lending work?" Like the traditional lending service provided by banks, DeFi lending, or decentralized finance lending, is provided through P2P decentralized applications instead of the banks. The DeFi lending systems enable anyone to borrow and lend money, allowing cryptocurrency owners to profit.

The DeFi lending protocol also enables lenders to earn interest on cryptocurrency holdings. DeFi lending allows people to become lenders much like banks, in contrast to banks' traditional loan processing mechanism. It is simple for someone to lend their possessions to others and charge interest on the loan. Like traditional banks' loan offices, DeFi lending is primarily based on lending pools, where users can add their assets and use smart contracts to assure timely distribution to borrowers.

Lenders must determine the type of interest because there are numerous techniques for allocating interest to investors. Because each lending pool has a different approach to borrowing, borrowers must also do their part by researching the lending pools.

What distinguishes DeFi lending from traditional lending?

The conventional financial system offers spot trading, margin trading, borrowing, and lending. However, the DeFi ecosystem has evolved and can now provide comparable financial services.

One of the key distinctions between DeFi and conventional financing is that the former requires a time-consuming process and ongoing customer status checks, while the latter does not. DeFi, on the other hand, issues loans more quickly if the borrower complies with all collateral conditions.

The borrower and the lender benefit from the smart contracts handling the entire vetting process. When compared to traditional loan markets, DeFi lending often provides superior returns.

What Advantages Does DeFi Lending Offer Users?

DeFi lending mainly motivates participants to deposit money in exchange for interest. Compared to the rates provided by conventional banks, these interest rates are more profitable. In addition, there are many advantages to DeFi lending over the traditional loan system. These consist of the following:

Accountability: One of the major advantages of DeFi lending is accountability. Blockchain is a decentralized public ledger that can instantly provide records of all DeFi loans, together with the regulations and guidelines that allowed for their granting. When a specific DeFi loan is approved, the public distributed ledger primarily verifies all the financial transactions.

Lending analytics: The assessment and monitoring of the borrowing and lending market are primarily aided by having a fully computerized lending procedure. Another significant advantage of the DeFi loan procedure is lending analytics. The analytics for lending can be used to maximize resources. Additionally, it enables various DeFi lending platforms to learn more about the sources of loans to enhance the loan's performance.

Speed: DeFi loans are handled swiftly; once the loan is granted, the money is available immediately. Because the DeFi lending platforms are supported by cloud services that assist in identifying any fraud and other DeFi lending hazards, DeFi loans are completed more quickly.

Immutability and transparency: Any person connected to the network can quickly verify a blockchain. Decentralized blockchain technology allows DeFi lending to guarantee transparency by ensuring all transactions' validity.

Permissionless: Anyone with a DeFi crypto loan wallet has permissionless, public access to decentralized lending. Regardless of one's financial situation or location, one can use DeFi applications created on blockchain networks.

Programmability and interoperability: One is to ensure that the DeFi lending protocols integrate and complement one another using the connected software stack. Additionally, smart contracts allow for the creation of financial instruments and digital assets and are highly programmable.

Asset management: Users can act as the only custodians of their crypto assets thanks to DeFi lending protocols and crypto wallets like Metamask, Gnosis Safe, and Argent. Additionally, it enables users can safely interact with decentralized applications and use services like purchasing, selling, earning interest on investments, and moving cryptocurrency.

Savings : Users can increase their earnings and use interest-bearing accounts by connecting to various lending platforms.

Constraints in Decentralized Lending

The advantages of DeFi lending are heavily emphasized in several well-known debates on decentralized finance. To properly assess its potential, it is also essential to highlight the drawbacks. The following is a list of significant obstacles that you may experience quickly after implementing DeFi lending:

Uncertainty: A DeFi lending process may immediately inherit instability from the host blockchain if there is any instability while hosting a blockchain. The Ethereum blockchain is undergoing several upgrades, and the risk may result, for instance, from errors made during the PoW consensus transition to the new Ethereum 2.0 POS system.

Scalability: DeFi lending may have trouble keeping the host blockchain scalable for several reasons. DeFi transactions, for instance, require additional time for confirmation. The DeFi protocol transactions could also increase costs during the congestion period, which overall impacts scalability.

Shared obligation: Among all the drawbacks, the shared accountability element has the exact opposite effect on users. The DeFi initiatives decline to accept liability if you make a mistake, and they eliminate the intermediaries, leaving only the user in charge of their assets and funds. Therefore, solutions that can eliminate human error or mistakes are needed for the DeFi lending process.

Liquidity: Another vital element in blockchain protocols and DeFi-based lending is liquidity. The DeFi project's overall worth was around 77.29 billion US dollars as of June 2022. Refer to the infographic below for a better knowledge of the present TVL of the DeFi market:

Since June 2022, the market value of DeFi has decreased to less than 80 billion US dollars. Due to these critical adjustments, the crash for Terra (LUNA) and its stablecoin Terra USD (UST) on May 22 that resulted in coins like USDD losing their peg to the US dollar had a considerable influence on the DeFi market.

In addition, the DeFi loan procedure has been harmed by the decreasing crypto market. Therefore, the DeFi market is smaller and less reliable than conventional banking systems. Consequently, it may be challenging to place your trust in a sector that has liquidity issues.

Best DeFi Lending Sites

DeFi lending platforms provide loans to the general public or businesses without using intermediaries. DeFi lending methods allow users to generate stablecoins and earn interest on cryptocurrencies. The top platforms for DeFi financing are listed below:

Compound

A type of autonomous interest DeFi lending rates protocol used for open financial applications is called a compound. Users can earn a passive income immediately by depositing the cryptocurrency through borrowing and interest.

The Compound provides the ability to vote on choices like technological platform upgrades and the addition of new assets. You will receive a CToken as a crypto lender in proportion to the sum they contributed to the liquidity pool. Specific to the digital assets offered in the liquidity pool, a CToken is. Based on the corresponding interest rate of the liquidity pool, these tokens will accrue interest. On Compound, the top 3 markets are USDC, ETH, and DAI.

Aave

Another well-known DeFi loan site, Aave, debuted in 2020. It is an open-source, non-custodial liquidity protocol. Users of Aave can quickly deposit cryptocurrency into the liquidity pool in exchange for an equal number of ATokens.

With the aid of an inbuilt algorithm, interest rates are modified by the supply and demand dynamics in a specific liquidity pool. With more AToken holders, interest DeFi lending rates rise. To learn more about asset tokenization in blockchain, read this blog.

YouHodler

Another hybrid lending platform, YouHodler, offers stablecoin and fiat loans backed by cryptocurrency. YouHodler's goal is to assist people in ending passive holding (buy-and-hold technique) and fully utilizing cryptocurrency. YouHodler, a Swiss company, provides an exchange policy as well.

The marketplace accepts money, cryptocurrencies, and stablecoins. Compared to other lending services, YouHodler offers lower interest rates. Compared to other lending services like crypto.com, Binance, Celsius Network, and BlockFi, the current interest rate is better at 12.3%.

Uniswap

A decentralized cryptocurrency exchange, Uniswap is built on the Ethereum network. One of the most significant benefits of this platform is that users can exchange smart contracts to control their money. A factory smart contract can also make it simple to list new coins on the exchange. Using Uniswap, users can quickly exchange their ERC-20 tokens.

MakerDAO

You can only borrow DAI tokens from the decentralized lending platform known as MakerDAO. Stablecoins like DAI are linked to the US dollar. You may quickly borrow DAI through Maker while pledging BAT or ETH as security. MakerDAO users are urged to participate in the operating profits, which are simply the network's interest rates. A user may borrow DAI up to 66% of the value of the collateral.

What does DeFi Lending's Future Hold?

DeFi lending has expanded dramatically over the past few years. 2023 is sure to present new obstacles, but there are also many great opportunities. As more investors engage in cutting-edge financial technologies, several initiatives based on DeFi are picking up steam. Flash loans are becoming increasingly popular, which is anticipated to rise in the coming days.

On the other hand, Flash loans have experienced relatively few issues recently while being more susceptible to suspicious and fraudulent activity. Despite all the technological advances, DeFi loan processing still has problems with security and financial fraud. It is anticipated that it will be renovated and enhanced in the future.

The existing financial system is experimental, young, and plagued with issues, particularly scalability and security. However, we continue to think that the best is yet to come. Ethereum 2.0 may provide a solution for the DeFi sector. Through the Sharding idea, Ethereum 2.0 can increase the network's scalability.

By sharding, the database can be broken into more manageable chunks for consumers. As DeFi lending continues to give consumers financial independence and user-friendly platforms, the latest technological developments will continue transforming how businesses and individuals share information, communicate, and use financial options.

Use a blockchain development company like Appinevntiv's special decentralized financial development services, and get ready to see a change in your organization. Today, get more information from our specialists about the DeFi ecosystem and how DeFi financing functions.

Key features in this chapter

- There are many advantages to DeFi lending over the conventional loan system.
- A type of autonomous interest DeFi lending rates protocol used for open financial applications is called a compound.
- Any change in the asset price after the assets have been deposited in the pool results in an impermanent loss.
- The DeFi lending platforms, sometimes referred to as the DeFi lending protocols, enable customers to obtain a DeFi loan.

4

AFTER FTX: IF DEFI FIXES ITS PROBLEMS, IT CAN BECOME WIDELY USED

Investors are turning to noncustodial platforms due to the collapse of FTX and other centralized platforms in 2022. Concerns concerning unregulated centralized platforms have increased significantly with the fall of the now-bankrupt bitcoin exchange FTX.

Investors have recently expressed serious worries about centralized decision-making without checks and are beginning to wonder how safe it is to store one's money on these exchanges. It was discovered that FTX was using the crypto assets customers had contributed to offset its business losses while holding $1 billion in a customer's fund.

Furthermore, according to recent research, the failure of several cryptocurrency exchanges over the past ten years has permanently removed 1.2 million Bitcoin ($16,536) from circulation, or nearly 6% of the total amount.

Investors already losing faith in these centralized trading businesses are panicking due to the disclosure of unethical practices by FTX in its bankruptcy petition. Following the FTX debacle, exchange outflows have reached all-time highs of 106,000 BTC each month. The need for more confidence in centralized exchanges (CEXs) has driven investors into self-custody and decentralized finance platforms.

Users have taken money out of cryptocurrency exchanges to trade monies and used noncustodial solutions. On November 11, the day FTX filed for bankruptcy, Uniswap, one of the ecosystem's biggest decentralized exchanges (DEX), recorded a considerable increase in trading volume.

The collapse of FTX served as a stimulus for a noticeable increase in volume in DEX trading. Last week, Uniswap had a 24-hour trading volume of over $1 billion, outpacing many centralized exchanges during the same period.

The failure of centralized organizations like FTX, according to Aishwary Gupta, DeFi chief of staff at Polygon, has undoubtedly served to remind users of the value of DeFi:

Code is the law for DeFi-centric systems; therefore, they are immune to unethical commercial practices. Users undoubtedly are aware of it as well. Following the collapse of FTX, Uniswap overtook Coinbase to overtake Binance as the largest Ethereum trading platform. Corruption and poor management have no place in decentralized platforms since they are managed by transparent, auditable smart contracts rather than humans.

According to statistics from Token Terminal, the daily trading volume of perpetual exchanges hit $5 billion, the most excellent daily trading volume since the Terra crisis in May 2022.

To better understand investor behavior in the wake of the FTX crisis and how it has affected their platform, Cointelegraph contacted PalmSwap, a decentralized perpetual exchange. Palmswap's co-founder and chief product officer, Bernd Stöckl, told Cointelegraph that trading volumes had increased significantly on the exchange.

"With the demise of FTX, DeFi usage will undoubtedly increase. According to rumors, centralized exchanges like Crypto.com, Gate.io, Gemini, and others are in deep trouble.

He continued, "With so many CEXs failing, trust in custodial wallets is very low, and more people will undoubtedly embrace the benefits of DeFi."

Since traders are generally reluctant to trust CEXs with their assets, Elie Azzi, co-founder and DeFi infrastructure supplier of VALK, feels the surge in DEX volumes could signal the start of a longer-term trend. According to him, DEXs are evolving considerably more quickly than their equivalents, with execution and settlement speeds on some chains approaching instantaneity. The current tendency is for DEXs to enhance CEXs' usability and user interface (UI) while strengthening their internal logic. Along with the distinctive qualities that DEXs bring, such as self-custody, the capacity to conduct transactions from one's wallet, and the ability to maintain control over private keys.

He continued by saying that while CEX platforms would experience stricter regulations and transparency campaigns, this transparency "would exist presumptively in complete DeFi. Instead, there would be no need for anyone to entrust CEXs with assets because all activity, including trading and liquidity provision, would be tracked in real-time on-chain."

DeFi's struggle with targeted hacks

In the wake of centralized exchange failures, DeFi protocols have experienced a noticeable uptick; nonetheless, the developing ecosystem itself has become a top target for hackers in 2022. Almost 97% of cryptocurrency stolen in the first quarter of 2022 has been taken from DeFi protocols, according to statistics from the crypto analytics company Chainalysis.

The Ronin network vulnerability from March, which cost $620 million in losses, is one of the most significant DeFi exploits of 2022. The Nomad bridge was breached for $190 million, and the Wormhole bridge hack cost $320 million. In

October, cryptocurrency assets worth $718 million were stolen from 11 different DeFi protocols.

According to Jordan Kruger, CEO, and co-founder of DeFi staking protocol Vesper Finance, the majority of attacks in the DeFi ecosystem have taken place on cross-chain bridges. They shouldn't be regarded as DeFi exploits.

Bridge assaults have made up a sizable percentage of such exploits (around $3 billion this year). Infrastructure, not so much "DeFi," is what bridges are; this number is by orders of magnitude dwarfed by CEX losses. Nevertheless, due to its capacity to iterate more quickly than centralized alternatives, DeFi will advance and increase security more quickly. This is comparable to how Linux benefited immensely from an open-source strategy, built a solid reputation for security, and had spectacular adoption.

DeFi is based on the principles of real decentralization, and smart contracts are frequently used to automate the decision-making process. Despite DeFi's efforts to exclude human participation, flaws still exist, whether from improperly coded smart contracts or data breaches.

While emerging DeFi technology is vulnerable to some bugs and issues, it is important to keep in mind that most hacks "have been related to either lending or cross-chain bridging," according to Lang Mei, CEO of AirDAO, speaking with Cointelegraph. To reduce the possibility of exploitable code in their decentralized apps, he offered further steps that developers should take. For example, "White hat hacking, bug bounty programs, and testnet incentivization are all excellent tools to help discover and repair problems."

From a team standpoint, they can also draw in and keep consumers, so it is a win-win situation. Decentralizing governance power through distributing the token supply and security measures like multi-signature wallets is also crucial.

Co-founder of the community-owned DApp platform Peaq Till Wendler told Cointelegraph that it's making smart contacts and design utterly free of human-related defects is challenging.

The DeFi space is definitely in better shape than it used to be. On the other hand, even the most rigorous smart contract security audit only gets you so far. He noted that specific attacks emerge from how smart contracts interact with each other in the larger ecosystem and not only from their inherent design problems.

DeFi can benefit from advancements in security technology, according to Mitchell Amador, CEO of the bug bounty protocol Immunefi, who told Cointelegraph that "a big explosion of security tech is being silently constructed in the background to handle the security challenge from all perspectives."

DeFi may eventually supplant centralized platforms due to advancements in security and user experience (UX), as well as the inherent transparency of DeFi. Still, this dynamic also depends on the arbitrary nature of laws, "Added Amador.

Undoubtedly, a sign of the times is the demise of centralized platforms in 2022 and the emergence of noncustodial and DeFi services. But many in the cryptocurrency industry believe that the lack of comprehension and due diligence on the part of the crypto investors was the most crucial component in the FTX fiasco.

Numerous cryptocurrency experts have long promoted self-custody and the usage of a decentralized platform. The co-founder of the Umbria Network, Barney Chambers, told Cointelegraph that the cryptocurrency industry "remains the untamed, wild west of finance." Some guidelines to ensure your money is secure include: never use a hardware wallet to store your keys, connect your wallet to a Website you don't trust, or ask for advice online from an unidentified stranger. Always [do your research]!

Investors must now demand from the parties they are investing in that they provide transparent and understandable information on all accounting. They must rely on noncustodial solutions for wallets and trading platforms to ensure their money is safe.

Noncustodial services need to be the way of the future for investors, according to Darren Mayberry, ecosystem head of the decentralized operating system dappOS.

"Accountability and audits should be regular operating practices for all investors, and due diligence and fact-checking are inherent components of the business." On the other hand, he said that noncustodial wallets are the most dependable type of storage since they place all duty on the owner, eliminating any potential counterparty concerns.

DeFi platforms may have their dangers and vulnerabilities. Industry watchers believe that with sufficient due diligence and a decrease in human error, the developing ecosystem of DEX platforms might become the preferred choice over CEX platforms.

DeFi is the Solution to the FTX Crisis, but we Need to Improve our Communication

DeFi provides a path ahead amid the roiling crypto liquidity maelstrom. Those of us trying to incorporate decentralized finance into our ideas have found the events of the previous two weeks very disheartening. Unintentional users suffered an injury and, in some cases, have lost all their savings. Court papers and leaked documents reveal the extent of fraud, carelessness, and wrongdoing at FTX, and the crisis has already damaged the trustworthiness of our entire ecosystem.

The sequence of events is ironic because DeFi envisions a financial system in which what transpired at FTX is not merely implausible but also impossible.

The general public needs to be made aware that an actual on-chain decentralized protocol would make it impossible for user funds to be misused at FTX, where it appears that FTX secretly moved user monies to Alameda Research, which has led to a loss of credibility. An open, immutable blockchain would make it difficult for FTX to hide its insolvency, as they appear to have done by using creative accounting. A genuine permissionless DeFi protocol would not be able to discriminate against users in this way, as FTX did when the exchange conducted business with Bahamians last week while it was collapsing. And, most significantly, users of a self-custody DeFi protocol would not be subject to the same catastrophe that may result in the total loss of cash for FTX users.

DeFi could be better in its current state, and there are drawbacks to smart contract risk, technical knowledge gaps, and decentralized organizations that move slowly. While this is happening, a few controlled, centralized organizations have proven they can be beneficial and dependable DeFi partners.

The most harmful condition, then, is not totally centralized or fully decentralized organizations but organizations that pass for DeFi while giving in to the same inclinations that DeFi is meant to correct. Because of this, we must explain the distinction between DeFi and centralized finance. The DeFi community may be aware that FTX was not a DeFi initiative, but most new users, the general public, regulators, and politicians cannot distinguish between the two.

It is important to emphasize that genuine DeFi lacks the immutable, decentralized, transparent, and permissionless properties of FTX, making it impossible for it to experience the failures of FTX.

DeFi also needs to be more readily available. Up to a million consumers, many of whom used the platform because it was simple and user-friendly, may be impacted by the failure of FTX.com. Our responsibility is to provide the dApps, wallets, and instructional resources that will make it simple and secure for these individuals to sign up for DeFi.

Many members have already made these arguments of our community on Twitter and in crypto media. Yet further action is required.

We must communicate outside Crypto Twitter as we deal with future government intrusions, obstinate investors, and traumatized users. We must communicate with traditional media, authorities, institutional partners, and ordinary consumers. We must make it evident that what we are creating is the solution to financial fraud, social exclusion, and consumer abuse throughout history—not only to the wrong-doing at FTX.

Although this time is sad for everyone who cares about DeFi, it also presents a chance to make clear who we are and what we stand for. DeFi must be comprehended and judged according to its qualities. If we are held accountable for the transgressions of centralized finance, it is because we neglected to distinguish and emphasize the significance of our work. Nothing less than DeFi's future is at risk.

FTX Failure Highlights Value of Defi and DEXs

This indicates in the context of cryptography that you are not the owner of your crypto if you do not own the private keys. Many people recently suffered due to learning a lesson the hard way. Everyone was reminded of the need for self-custody of money and the dangers of putting their confidence in centralized institutions by the collapse of FTX, which stole billions of customers' dollars.

While authorities are stepping up strong measures on running crypto companies, the media has dubbed this as the end of cryptocurrency and said to "let crypto burn." Many claims that the FTX meltdown seriously harms the cryptocurrency market and demonstrates how unreliable and unstable this sector is.

But let's stand back for a moment. Just what is crypto? Bitcoin is recognized as the first cryptocurrency, which serves as a reminder of what it is: an electronic currency that can only be used peer-to-peer, allowing payments to be sent over the internet directly from one party to another without going through a bank.

Think about it. "Not using a financial institution. Users may store their cash in their self-custody and conduct peer-to-peer transactions without using an intermediary, thanks to the inherent characteristics of blockchain technology and encryption.

Where does the crypto industry stand in light of the FTX debacle? Does this spell the end of cryptocurrency, or will it advance on-chain activity, DeFi, self-custody, and code trust? Let's start now.

FTX

With the demise of FTX, millions of user dollars are lost. Due to exposure to FTX, other firms offering centralized crypto services (CeFi) are impacted, and some are forced to shut down their businesses. FTX was in the cryptocurrency sector, yet this is not a crypto failure.

Human error, greed, manual transaction obscuration, and manual client money theft are to blame. It involves a pleasant and cunning person who gains trust by projecting a positive image while running one of the most significant financial and cryptocurrency frauds.

The Sam Bankman-Fried product was purchased. People enjoyed the picture he painted of a clever millionaire, geek and philanthropist, appearing on the Forbes cover. He was trusted not just by simple crypto retail users but also by seasoned investors, powerful funds, and high net worth people. Many wanted to touch a piece of his business and be a part of it.

People who put their faith in Sam Bankman-Fried were duped. But were blockchain and cryptocurrencies a betrayal of them?

Is the future in DeFi?

CeFi was practical, and many institutional and retail crypto customers trusted it and were used to its white-glove service. Along with FTX, other crypto CeFi players, like Genesis, BlockFi, etc., have begun to lose ground. These were the organizations that offered institutional-level financing as well as other services to institutional crypto players. As a result, institutional actors are also hurt by centralized entities' failures, in addition to retail customers.

Retail consumers who continue to utilize cryptocurrency are reminded of their responsibility and are moving toward adopting DEXs and DeFi platforms. The features and user-friendly interface of centralized exchanges made using them easy. But at this point, blockchain technology is sufficiently developed to provide comparable trading functionalities on decentralized exchanges to CEXs.

What worries the lending and borrowing markets? Compared to CEXs' equivalent services, DeFi is more readily available to retail consumers. DeFi is permissionless worldwide, so anybody with an internet connection may use it.

Institutional actors often seek transparency and have high capital efficiency. Why should they utilize CeFi when DeFi offers less expensive rates? No matter how great the support for a centralized party may be, why would you subject yourself to that danger if you don't have to?

In terms of transparency, loan underwriting, and risk, DeFi is setting the bar high. On-chain underwriting is more sophisticated; disclosing the holdings is necessary for oracles to know how the balance sheet is doing. DeFi has yet to evolve and mature fully, but because of the inherent characteristics of blockchain and cryptography, it is already far more transparent and safe than CeFi.

The development of decentralized exchanges has progressed with technology. Nowadays, Layer 2 calculations and Zero-Knowledge technology are receiving much attention. All of this considerably raises the throughput of DEXs at a low gas cost while also elevating the capabilities of transaction matching. Trading using the Order Book and Limit Orders was previously available on decentralized exchanges that, before Uniswap, mainly employed AMM (Automated Market Maker) processes.

All operations, whether they include a DAO repurchase, a public sale, or the conversion of tokens, may be revealed to the community since DEXs are fundamentally transparent. A big open market with little custodial risk and fresh arbitrage possibilities, DEXs have already attracted the attention of professional market makers.

The industry is developing and moving ahead in the wake of the FTX and other CeFi disasters. Market players must utilize technology effectively and take self-custody seriously. Code governs the whole ecosystem and is already a regulation in and of itself for smart contracts. Defi has complete transparency as opposed to the closed books of centralized institutions.

Blockchain offers resources for a transparent, decentralized, permissionless, and decentralized financial environment. After becoming used to centralized financial systems, it may be challenging to adapt, but ultimately, individuals and businesses will relocate to where their money is most effective and safe.

The Reason Decentralized Crypto Platforms Survived the Crash

Toward the end of 2021, the cryptocurrency market reached record highs before collapsing in 2022. There was a significant decline in value from $2.9 trillion in worth in November 2021 to around $800 billion a year later. Leading crypto lenders and exchanges also failed when the market value fell.

Many of these platforms are now being sued and accused of significant misbehavior, including fraud claims against Celsius. Voyager Digital is being sued collectively for fraud and the sale of unregistered securities to its customers. BlockFi reached a settlement with the SEC and 32 states over related allegations, is still subject to a class action lawsuit, and finally declared bankruptcy.

Two class-action lawsuits have been filed against the co-founder of Terraform Labs, the company that developed the algorithmic stablecoin TerraUSD. An arrest order has been issued in South Korea. Now, the newly bankrupt centralized exchange FTX is being investigated for "severe fraud and mismanagement," Its co-founder Sam Bankman-Fried is being closely examined by Congress, prosecutors, and civil lawsuits.

Some believe that the latest upheaval portends the demise of cryptocurrency, and they see the declines as proof that bitcoin is a fraud. These failures, however, did not affect the base of cryptocurrency. Instead, they represent a particular market sector dominated by secretive, centralized organizations that made it hard for their clients to comprehend the dangers they were incurring.

Additionally, the relative simplicity with which users could move their cryptocurrency assets across platforms fueled a fierce level of competitiveness that forced companies to continually offer offers that seemed to be better and better while carrying higher and higher levels of concealed risk.

In this respect, such a financial disaster isn't novel; fierce competition in marketplaces with opaque goods has often resulted in financial failures. Ironically, although easier competition is desirable in markets, it may have worsened the issues in this case.

But at the same time, the centralized institutions that failed stand in stark contrast to other crypto market sectors, such as those built on decentralized protocols that run on defined algorithms and have high levels of transparency. These platforms operated consistently while exposed to the same market dynamics and upheaval.

This section describes some economic variables that drove this series of events. Then, as decentralized finance develops, it could provide a way to leverage the advantages of competitive crypto infrastructure with stronger consumer protection.

Competition and opacity in Web3

To comprehend how we ended here, you must understand why competition in the crypto/Web3 space behaves differently from conventional business settings. Data and assets are kept behind "walled gardens" on well-established Web 2.0 platforms and in conventional financial institutions, making data and asset transfers expensive and time-consuming. Even material developed on Websites like Twitter and Facebook is challenging to extract, and once it is, it comes in a file format that is tough to transfer to another Website. However, relatively few customers are looking for better banking alternatives due to the perceived high switching costs associated with consumer banking.

In contrast, moving a user's assets around is straightforward since digital assets are handled and maintained on open, interoperable blockchains. Users have ownership over their assets and often do not even need to tell a platform when they leave for a rival, making the cost of moving platforms relatively minimal. Platforms must thus engage in severe competition to retain users and attract new ones.

Economically speaking, more competition will benefit customers by lowering platform costs, raising platform quality, and empowering and safeguarding the purchasing public. To promote consumer welfare, authorities and politicians specifically support competition.

In fact, we have seen these factors at work in several crypto marketplaces. New platforms for trading fungible and non-fungible crypto tokens have been developed. By providing innovative features and reduced fees, they have effectively seized market share from incumbents by capitalizing on customers' low switching costs.

Users may evaluate transaction possibilities frictionlessly across many platforms via aggregators, and the platforms often compete with one another by giving users larger shares of governance tokens and other benefits. Another example is "yield farming," in which customers utilize open data on available options and minimal switching costs to reallocate their cash algorithmically and instantaneously to the items with the best return.

But there's a problem: Certain crypto goods and services are opaque and may need to be simplified for the typical customer to grasp. Intense competition may produce problems when customers need help grasping an item because they need more skills or be provided with crucial information. In particular, rival businesses might give customers more alluring bargains while hiding possible hazards.

This dynamic is not exclusive to cryptocurrency—markets for everything from used automobiles and financial management to insurance and medical care experience it. But since the assets they deal with are innovative and perhaps inherently complicated, hiding potential issues may be particularly feasible on specific cryptocurrency platforms. Risk is increased by the fact that consumer protection and transparency regulations are still in their infancy.

In such situations, corporations may increasingly provide desirable product features while concealing rising underlying costs and hazards as competition heats up.

When economic forces turn negative

There is a lot of history behind fierce competition, opaque financial products, and unsustainable rates. For instance, in the banking industry, deregulation in the 1970s and 1980s boosted competition, reduced profit margins, amplified risk-taking by banks, and increased bank failures. Recent studies have shown that banks often construct their financial products for families to raise the headline interest rate while also raising the complexity and risk of the products.

Of course, widespread fraud in the mortgage securitization sector was a hallmark of the 2008 financial crisis. This conduct was primarily influenced by increasing market competitiveness as originators dropped credit criteria and participated in predatory lending to boost profits.

While competition may and should benefit consumers, history has repeatedly shown how severe rivalry in the financial markets fosters the growth of dangerous and complex goods, albeit for a short time, by luring customers in with unbelievable bargains that will ultimately go bad.

This snowball dynamic is again shown in the context of many centralized platforms by the most recent collapse of the cryptocurrency market. Without adequately disclosing the tremendous leverage and risk they used to obtain such returns, Celsius and Voyager Digital, two significant centralized, retail-facing lending systems now in bankruptcy, provided extraordinarily enticing rewards on consumer deposits.

To boost interest in Terraform Labs' stablecoin, TerraUSD, which crashed later in the year, Anchor, a lending platform established and owned by Terraform Labs, promised depositors unsustainable returns. One of the most centralized cryptocurrency exchanges, FTX, apparently used client cash to cover the losses of its sister business, the hedge fund Alameda Research, while enticing consumers with discounts on crypto asset trading.

Small changes in yield promises might result in significant capital movements in a highly competitive business where clients can switch financial providers. Such actions increase the incentives to artificially enhance client terms, especially when the financial products are complicated and opaque.

Market competition may push out efficient businesses. However, the opaque nature of centralized crypto money made it possible for unproductive companies to compete by providing short-term enticing but ultimately unsustainable goods. Unfortunately, as we have seen, such organizations can accumulate substantial assets before the inevitable collapse of their business models.

For cryptocurrency firms and individuals, the last year has been full of challenging lessons. But the repeated stress testing has shown what works. Users will have additional possibilities to benefit from DeFi's exceptional transparency as it develops. They should thus be better able to take full advantage of the fierce platform competition that blockchain architecture makes possible.

Key features in this chapter

- Investors are turning to noncustodial platforms due to the collapse of FTX and other centralized platforms in 2022.
- Since traders are generally reluctant to trust CEXs with their assets, Elie Azzi, co-founder and DeFi infrastructure supplier of VALK, feels the surge in DEX volumes could signal the start of a longer-term trend.
- DeFi's struggle with targeted hacks. In the wake of centralized exchange failures, DeFi protocols have experienced a noticeable uptick; nonetheless, the developing ecosystem itself has become a top target for hackers in 2022.
- Almost 97% of all cryptocurrency stolen in the first quarter of 2022 has been taken from DeFi protocols, according to statistics from the crypto analytics company Chainalysis.
- Many in the cryptocurrency industry believe that the lack of comprehension and due diligence on the part of the crypto investors was the most critical component in the FTX fiasco.

5

UNDERSTANDING THE ADVANTAGES, RISKS, AND DIFFICULTIES OF DECENTRALIZED FINANCE

D ecentralized finance has shown an impressive adoption curve. By bypassing conventional interme- diaries, this new kind of blockchain-powered financing has seen locked-up assets increase from less than $1 billion in 2019 to more than $100 billion only two years later, bringing in at least one million investors in the process. The DeFi market is anticipated to reach $800 billion in 2022 as more institutional investors join the sector.

Unsurprisingly, proposals for regulation have been prompted by disrupting the conventional banking sector, but the DeFi market still needs to be explored. Financial institu- tions, for instance, are currently discussing in the US whose regulatory authority it fits under.

It's crucial for investors considering diversifying their port- folio into DeFi to comprehend the main components of the DeFi market. This section offers a general overview of DeFi's standard features, the industry's advantages and hazards, and any prospective future DeFi laws.

The advantages of DeFi

DeFi provides many practical use cases inaccessible to traditional fiat-based financial systems. Here are a few advantages of DeFi:

- DeFi is inclusive and permissionless. Anybody, everywhere, with a crypto wallet and an internet connection may use DeFi services. Additionally, users don't need to wait for bank transfers or pay traditional bank fees to conduct transactions or shift their assets. (However, other crypto-specific expenses, such as gas fees, could be necessary.)
- Transactions are real-time, interest rates are changed several times each minute, and the underlying blockchain is updated each time a transaction is completed.
- Transparency in all transactions. More than 90% of DeFi traffic is sent through the Ethereum blockchain, where other users broadcast and validate every transaction. Any user may see network activities thanks to this transaction data openness.
- Users may keep control of their funds by employing smart contract-based escrow or non-custodial cryptocurrency wallets.
- Smart contracts may be created to execute automatically depending on various factors and are extremely programmable.
- DeFi data is safe, auditable, and impervious to tampering owing to the usage of blockchain technology.
- A large number of DeFi protocols are open source. The code used to create Ethereum and other

projects is open-source, enabling anybody to access, check, and modify it. Without requesting permission, developers may quickly integrate various DeFi apps based on open-source technology to produce new financial services and products.

The risks of DeFi

DeFi provides interesting and novel financial freedoms, yet these freedoms are still in danger. These dangers consist of the following:

- DeFi technology is still in its infancy and has not yet undergone extensive scale-up stress testing. Money might disappear or be in danger. Compound, a DeFi platform, recently had a significant bug in which clients unintentionally received millions of dollars' worth of cryptocurrency.
- A lack of protection for consumers. In the absence of laws and restrictions, DeFi has prospered. But this implies that consumers often have little to no protection when anything goes wrong. No rules require capital reserves for DeFi service providers, and no state-run reimbursement programs include DeFi.
- Hackers are a threat. Although there is a danger of hacking in conventional banking, DeFi's extensive technical architecture, with its many possible points of failure, enhances the so-called attack surface that knowledgeable hackers may use. For instance, "white hat" hackers stole $610 million from the DeFi platform PolyNetwork in August 2021 by taking advantage of a smart contract vulnerability. Fortunately, every penny was repaid.

- There are strict collateral restrictions. Almost all DeFi lending transactions call for collateral that is at least equal to the loan's value, if not more. These conditions severely constrain the eligibility for various forms of DeFi loans.
- Private key requirements. Users using DeFi and cryptocurrencies must protect their wallets to keep their bitcoin holdings safe. This is a crucial prerequisite for multi-signature wallet users who are private investors with their own money and institutional investors. Private keys—lengthy, distinctive codes known only to the wallet's owners —are employed to do this. For instance, if a private investor misplaces their key, they are permanently unable to access their money.

Getting ready for possible regulation

Governmental agencies are rushing to determine who can regulate this new profession and what those restrictions would be as DeFi upends the financial services sector. DeFi's quick expansion can slow down in the coming years, depending on how it is implemented.

The Financial Action Task Force (FATF) is one significant participant in the fight against money laundering and is supported by the G7. DeFi platforms contain at least one legal or a person who is directing or influencing platform activity someplace, and the argument goes. Therefore, they are more decentralized than is commonly stated.

According to the FATF, virtual asset service providers (VASPs) are DeFi platforms that a single person or group still runs. A detailed plan for putting them under regulatory supervision currently exists. The FATF also proposes that a jurisdiction force a VASP to get engaged if an organization's specific DeFi platform needs to be administered.

The FATF's recommendations provide governments with a framework for creating DeFi regulations. This new approach is expected to lead to heated legal arguments between regulators and blockchain entrepreneurs over who controls or influences different DeFi protocols across countries.

Many DeFi platforms may step up their efforts to become fully decentralized by severing the connections between particular users and their platforms in preparation for future regulation.

Authorities will be careful to strike a balance between any regulatory control, implementing regulations like AML/CFT, and the financial advantages of DeFi innovation. Although the future may be uncertain, it will be crucial for DeFi investors to keep track of how regulatory frameworks governing this emerging financial industry change.

DeFi-ing the Rules for Decentralized Finance: Opportunities and Risks

The Force is a mystical energy field created by living creatures in the Star Wars universe that permeates everything and connects the galaxy. Jedi knights are the galactic peacekeepers thanks to their mastery of the Force, which endows them with superhuman powers. But how strong would the Jedi be if each "transaction" involving the Force had to go through a centralized system that imposed various taxes and was prone to delays?

Unfortunately, much of the conventional financial universe fits into the second scenario. When there is excessive friction in the financial system, it slows down transactions and drives up prices. At the Alpha Summit GLOBAL by CFA Institute last month, Campbell Harvey made the case that the era of centralized finance may end, and the age of decentralized finance may be just beginning. The finance professor at Duke University, co-author of DeFi and the Future of Finance, partner at Research Affiliates, and senior advisor believes that DeFi can alter the financial system and release a wave of economic activity.

According to Harvey, the old financial system has run on the same model for over a century. Everything depends upon the same commercial banks, exchanges, insurance companies, central banks, etc. The fundamental structure has remained constant and centralized despite technological advancements and related advances.

Fintech has recently sparked some disruption and assisted in lowering transaction costs. But because fintech is based on the same centralized financial architecture, there is a limit to how much efficiency can be gained and how low prices can be. That limit only exists with decentralized finance, according to Harvey. The present fintech boom will pass quickly because of this.

But why is DeFi such an inescapable force for transformation? Will there be that much improvement? What potential additional dangers might accompany it?

Binding the financial galaxy together

DeFi, in its simplest form, employs peer-to-peer networks to carry out transactions without intermediaries. The "smart contracts" that make up digital currencies like cryptocurrencies are self-executing algorithms built on the blockchain. Tokenization is a crucial component of DeFi. Tokens that serve as repositories of value that may be used in financial transactions can be created from virtual and actual assets. They also provide the holder a say in how a platform or protocol is run.

Why will DeFi change the way that money is made? Because it can address the five fundamental issues Harvey identifies with the current financial system: inefficiency, access restrictions, opacity, centralized control, and interoperability.

Eliminating intermediaries and fees are necessary to reduce inefficiencies. Harvey pointed out that a Western Union wire transfer cost 3% back in the 19th century. Even routine transactions now, such as using a debit card, frequently come with hefty fees more than a century later. Although a purchasing stock might appear quite simple, becoming an owner involves an intermediary and can take some time. DeFi allows for the simultaneous execution and settlement of trades.

A major issue facing the entire world is restricted access to the financial system. By removing these obstacles, millions of people could get access to the financial services they require. Estimates place the number of unbanked and underbanked individuals at 1.7 billion. Financial friction is the main challenge for many of these cohorts.

For instance, the exorbitant cost of capital discourages many small businesses from investing in initiatives that could spur economic growth by restricting access to loans with lower interest rates and instead offering lines of credit at significantly higher interest rates. Harvey asserts that DeFi can tackle the root causes of financial friction directly.

The idea that DeFi might reduce financial system obscurity may surprise the naysayers. For instance, in a letter to Gary Gensler, the head of the US SEC, in August 2021, US senator Elizabeth Warren urged him to regulate the cryptocurrency markets. He referred to DeFi as "very opaque."

Harvey, however, believes Warren has it wrong. The current financial system, he claimed, is opaque. DeFi uses open-source technology, so there is more transparency rather than less. Users, for instance, can view the code, the liquidity, and all the other details with a decentralized exchange. Contrarily, the conventional financial system has many flaws.

According to Harvey, when you visit a bank, you have no idea how healthy that bank is. And to lower your risk, you depend on our institutions like the FDIC. But our institutions have, at best, a questionable track record, and I'm not just referring to the 1930s. We can recall how many people dealt with failing banks during the global financial crisis.

Concentration and centralized control are crucial components of the modern financial system. Harvey uses the "market power" of business banks as an illustration. "That indicates that borrowing rates are higher than they ought to be and savings rates are lower than they ought to be. Maybe people are left out," he suggested. "And in decentralized systems, finance is different by definition. There is fierce competition.

He further said, "There is no differentiation between different participants in the [decentralized] arena. We are all equal,"

Interoperability is a structural issue in traditional finance that cannot be avoided. Different platforms and systems cannot connect due to various barriers. Someone may need to transfer funds from a bank account to open an account with an online trading platform. Before the new account is available to trade, the process could take several days.

It's significantly different with decentralized finance, Harvey added. "You go to an exchange, connect your wallet, and you're good to go. You have a wallet. This is a characteristic of the so-called Web 3.0 experience. Therefore, there are no login or passwords in Web 3.0. After connecting your wallet, you are prepared to travel. Your shopping is prepared. You are prepared to get paid. You are functioning. Furthermore, Web 3.0 can only exist with decentralized finance.

The dark side

DeFi will save the financial universe by overcoming oppressive centralization and inefficiencies. Wait a minute. DeFi has the potential to create novel threats as well as altered forms of existing threats. Harvey has identified five distinct types of risk related to smart contracts: oracle risk, custodial risk, environmental risk, and regulatory risk.

The risk associated with smart contracts: A smart contract is a self-executing, computerized contract between two parties. It's a blockchain platform algorithm that enables transactions to take place without the use of centralized systems or intermediaries.

Smart contracts are more exposed to cyber criminals than traditional systems secured by layers of security around a proprietary source since DeFi is open source. Due to their nature, smart contracts are open to several vulnerabilities, including logical mistakes, economic abuses (such as taking advantage of mispricing), flash loan assaults, and governance risk (for contracts with changing parameters). Security will advance when more vulnerabilities are discovered. Harvey added, "But it is incredibly risky right now.

The risk associated with Oracle: Smart contracts rely on external data, such as a price feed from a stock exchange. Blockchain oracles are the third-party services that offer the link. Certain actions necessary for a transaction cannot be done if the connection is disrupted, and the contract may fail.

Scaling risk: The consensus technique used by current DeFi platforms has slow transaction speeds. According to Harvey, Ethereum is "the dominant technology for decentralized finance" and can handle 15 transactions per second, and Visa has a processing speed of 65,000 transactions per second. And with bitcoin, the scaling issue is considerably more severe. You can only conduct transactions between persons using bitcoin, he claimed. "With the current version of Bitcoin, there is no way to have a smart contract."

Ethereum is already working to transition to a new and speedier consensus technique, despite the opinion of some that DeFi would never reach the scale of traditional financial networks. While this is happening, horizontal scaling and other cutting-edge strategies are being developed to lower transaction costs.

According to Harvey, people are currently complaining about the scalability issue and the rising costs of transactions on the Ethereum blockchain. And while it's true that they are high, all of these activities imply that they will go down significantly in the future.

Possession risk: Through a user's private key, self-custody in a digital wallet secures access to cryptocurrency assets. But a lost or stolen key might have fatal consequences. Harvey remarked, "If you lose your private key, you lose your cryptocurrency." What's more, the private key is a 256-bit random number. Private key theft horror stories have caused frightful headlines and significant financial losses. Third-party services have intervened to ensure users' access and protect private keys to ease their worries.

Regulatory risk: According to Harvey, "Regulators are currently battling with what to do with this new space...I believe they recognize the difficulty." However, achieving the ideal regulatory balance will be challenging. He also said, "If you want to minimize all risk and have very strict restrictions, that implies the technology is going abroad. The technology in question is not a national one. A worldwide technology exists. Therefore, you could do it just as easily from New York as from the Cayman Islands."

In other words, "regulators are in a bind." Harvey claimed that being too tough would stifle innovation. "If you're too tolerant, it becomes into the Wild West, where people are taken advantage of."

Building a new financial city

Harvey is one of many observers who think DeFi presents a chance to obtain a competitive advantage in a newly emerging new order. And these chances are uncommon in history. "Our current financial system is not being renovated in any way. We are extremely early in the process, 1% in, and can already see the skeletal framework of a new metropolis."

Ironically, this new financial system might resemble barter, a far older type of money. According to Harvey, when money was introduced, the barter system was upset, and market exchange improved significantly. Since decentralized finance redefines money, every asset can be tokenized.

A digital wallet might contain tokens connected to various assets, such as US currency, gold, and Apple shares. According to Harvey, "When I go to pay for something, I choose, perhaps I will use part of my Apple stock to pay for some groceries. The grocer might not want that, too. They desire different things. No issue. The Apple stock is seamlessly moved to a decentralized exchange and converted into anything the grocer desires. That is a swap done in a far more productive manner."

Harvey advises anyone who believes that rejecting DeFi is a choice to reconsider. He said, "Some traditional financial companies in your portfolio have a bullseye painted on them. And if [DeFi] continues to advance at the same rate as it has in recent years, the value of some businesses in your portfolio could significantly decline. So, could you give it some thought? Despite not being in, you still receive negative exposure."

Opportunities and Challenges for Banks in a Decentralized Finance Environment

Decentralized exchanges (DEX) and automated asset management are examples of use cases for decentralized finance. Obstacles to the widespread adoption of DeFi applications still exist, including a lack of legislative clarity, public awareness of how to handle DeFi applications or even the inapplicability of contracts.

In light of this, we will demonstrate why financial institutions should give their clients access to digital assets and DeFi business models as well as the difficulties they must face. Existing direct access to digital assets is a necessary condition for providing decentralized finance. Positioning options for regulated institutions and actual opportunities and difficulties will be given based on real-world experiences.

Opportunities

As stated in this series' first piece, the prospective returns from digital assets or DeFi business models are significantly higher than those from conventional investment strategies. Decentralized finance is appealing to financial organizations due to the interest it generates from investors. The latter can attract new clients by extending their offering to include digital assets and related services and obtain larger margins for their services due to the higher earning potential. Three stages that build on one another make up the extension of the service:

- Adding DeFi tokens to the digital asset offering
- Taking part in DeFi business models
- Providing asset maintenance to third parties

In the framework of decentralized finance, a fundamental offering of digital assets, such as trading and custody of digital assets, serves as the basis for creating new revenue streams.

Increasing the current selection of digital assets

Financial institutions' initial distrust of digital assets has gradually decreased over the past few years, and the number of institutions with comparable offerings is increasing. The National Association of German Cooperative Banks is one instance of a company developing prototypes for digital assets offering that might be made available to 18 million consumers.

Many retail and private banks in Switzerland have already entered the market with such an offering, including the transaction bank Incore, the online bank Swissquote, and the crypto banks SEBA Bank & Sygnum. Many conventional financial institutions, however, now give their clients access to digital assets.

Since these securities can easily be integrated into the institutions' existing technical infrastructure, most of this is still by indirect access, for instance, exchange-traded products (ETPs) or certificates that invest in digital assets. However, some banks are already working on direct access to digital assets. The so-called "blue chips," Bitcoin or Ethereum, are frequently included in this list of digital assets.

The product line can then be expanded to include more coins and a wide array of services, including, in addition to staking, things like lending these digital assets.

Access to DeFi applications and tokens is the logical next step. For instance, a bank may add DeFi tokens to the direct access to digital assets it provides its clients through online or mobile banking. These guarantee an income prospect for investors through the underlying decentralized financial application and price increases of the protocol or governance tokens (e.g., revenue as a liquidity provider in the context of decentralized exchanges; more details follow in the next section).

DeFi tokens also allow investors to create a topic-specific digital asset portfolio similar to traditional investing themes (e.g., biotech, mobility, or technology). To prevent the dilution of DeFi tokens, an offer of DeFi tokens is best made in conjunction with direct involvement in DeFi business models (more on this in the next section).

Participating in DeFi business

Decentralized lending and automated asset management (AAM), two business concepts underlie DeFi, offer yet another chance to boost profits for investors and the financial institution. From an investor's standpoint, this typically produces larger returns than comparable goods from the conventional financial sector. For instance, lending USDC in a DeFi setting can result in up to 7.25% returns. Such an offer is best compared to the financial institution's asset management mission in the traditional financial sector.

In this case, a bank actively manages investors' assets by predetermined criteria without getting the investor's consent on every investment choice. Investors profit from the bank's investing knowledge and, ideally, from its capacity to produce returns, while the bank benefits from a steady stream of management fees.

When this idea is implemented in DeFi, the financial institution actively manages digital assets and invests them in related DeFi applications per the investor's wishes. When lending is decentralized, the financial institution lends money on the client's behalf. Lenders benefit from the lending pool's increased liquidity by providing it and are compensated with the delivered digital asset (e.g., USDC). These resources may be held by them or lent out in return.

The latter, known as "yield farming," seeks to maximize profit by supplying liquidity for decentralized lending. The financial institution does not invest digital assets in automated asset management, where the investment process is automated, as the name suggests. Instead, they are transferred to the smart contract's vault and invested in other DeFi applications by the smart contract's investment strategy. Digital assets are transferred to liquidity pools (decentralized exchanges, DEX) or lending pools (borrowing-lending), for instance, and provide returns. These returns are given to investors after deducting the AAM fee.

In the case of decentralized exchanges, a liquidity provider token (LPT) may be given to liquidity providers by DeFi applications in exchange for the liquidity they have provided. These tokens can then create additional rewards for investors by being added to a liquidity or lending pool.

This investing technique is known as "liquidity mining," which entails continuously supplying liquidity in digital assets and liquidity providers or lending tokens in different DeFi applications to maximize one's return. As the total supply rises, the value of existing tokens is diminished by the creation of LPT or lending tokens via the DeFi program. Therefore, continuing to lend or invest in the tokens makes sense.

But why do financial institutions need to be aware of these business models? A bank can not only provide a secure location for investors to store their private keys for their digital assets during the custody period, but it can also invest those funds in DeFi applications, opening up new business options for investors.

In addition to giving customers a consolidated view of their assets, the financial institution offers them a stress-free package, so they don't have to worry about dealing with separate protocols and investment plans. This service adds value to the client's experience, and thus it can be priced with confidence.

. . .

Increasing the range of services offered

Asset servicing for third parties is a third option in the context of DeFi and financial institutions. As previously indicated, institutional adoption is fueled by direct investments in digital assets and traditional securities based on those assets, such as derivatives like exchange-traded vehicles (ETPs).

By acquiring the derivative rather than the actual assets, these derivatives give investors indirect access to digital assets. Per the specifications in the securities prospectus, investments are made in various digital assets, such as Bitcoin. Each security receiving an International Securities Identification Number (ISIN) can be mapped in the custody account of most banks like any other security.

The investor can handle digital assets without prior experience dealing with digital assets (e.g., concerning the safekeeping of the private key, triggering a blockchain transaction, etc.). Digital assets packaged in this way have been quite popular recently. They are now available through blockchain startups and conventional financial institutions, such as Switzerland's Leonteq (e.g., the Austrian crypto exchange Bitpanda).

These businesses depend upon asset servicing services offered by a custodian for such an offering, such as asset custody or trade value computation. Their operations have their roots in the conventional securities industry. DeFi presents new product prospects for issuers, such as a security that participates in the business models of DeFi applications if it is added to the list of investable digital assets.

Financial institutions take custody of and actively manage digital assets (for more information, see the opportunity "Participating in DeFi business models"). However, since a different legal entity, such as a special purpose vehicle (SPV) or fund, is involved in the case of an ETP, compared to a direct investment, an additional counterparty risk occurs, which investors should be aware of.

The issue of how many of these products should be available on the market and whether implementation should be handled by specialized service providers or by the banks themselves subsequently emerges in practical implementation.

Opportunities: a first analysis

Financial institutions can be well-prepared for the future, where decentralized finance is more extensively used by pursuing one of the options above. Financial institutions are well-suited to map new regulations since they already have to adhere to various regulations in their core business, especially in light of the growing regulation of digital assets.

From the investor's perspective, this may induce a leap of faith in the professional and legal handling of digital assets and DeFi apps. The present Web 3.0 advances favor businesses that address potential repercussions on their business strategy early on. In digital assets and DeFi, most transactions in a Web 3.0 environment will be carried out using digital assets in a decentralized manner. As a result, central financial institutions' function in processing transactions must be reconsidered.

The reason financial institutions have yet to take full advantage of these prospects is now under doubt. DeFi applications have several difficulties that need to be fully overcome, like other investments that have promised returns.

Challenges

Creating revenue sources for DeFi applications now presents several difficulties. The ability of DeFi to disrupt the current financial sector, which is based on centralized intermediaries, is the most fundamental of these. Another problem is that DeFi applications are mostly uncontrolled, which presents difficulties for institutions under supervision.

Disruption of business model by DeFi

Decentralized finance will likely displace the current business models of central intermediaries like brokers, banks, and stock exchanges. Smart contracts' automated handling of complex transactions puts existing financial industry institutions in jeopardy and may make them unnecessary.

Without the need for centralized intermediaries and with a faster settlement time, blockchain-based smart contracts can reach a comparable degree of trust in financial transactions. DeFi transactions should become more efficient and cost-effective once intermediaries are no longer required. Additional drivers for the growth of DeFi apps include the general population's growing embrace of digital assets and world trends like Web 3.0. As a result, the further spread of DeFi applications poses a threat to conventional business models that include numerous central intermediates.

Banks can identify the potential for their business model to be disrupted early and develop measures by looking at DeFi applications. The creation of expertise, the discovery of efficiency and effectiveness potentials in the delivery of their services, or the organized investigation of market developments in partnership with pertinent market actors from the blockchain/DeFi industry are examples of initial measures.

Banks could position themselves as trusted mediators at the interface of DeFi business models or as custodians of digital assets, including DeFi (e.g., when switching from fiat to digital assets and vice versa). In conclusion, banks can take a proactive role in shaping DeFi and contribute to the transition.

Knowledge and techniques for handling DeFi

Different skills and knowledge are required in various areas of a financial institution to deal with digital assets in a regulated framework. The technical custody of digital assets must be managed, on-chain due diligence (OCDD) must be conducted, and the compliance team must evaluate its results. A risk management framework must be developed to identify and describe the risks associated with DeFi transactions and their effects on the rest of the business.

From a compliance standpoint, the OCDD, in particular, is very important for banks because blockchain transactions also require adherence to compliance rules similar to those used for currency transactions. The transaction history of the questioned digital assets is checked during OCDD, namely which wallets these digital assets were transferred via in the past. Transactions on a blockchain may be tracked back to the first block made since public blockchains are highly transparent.

Dealing with DeFi necessitates the development of additional abilities, such as comprehension of DeFi business models, analysis of unique protocols, and evaluation of smart contract quality. Recruiting experts can be difficult and expensive since more financial institutions are dealing with the issue of digital assets and because such talents are in demand in the job market.

Infrastructure

Safekeeping, private keys for digital assets, is crucial to any decentralized finance product or digital asset. This issue should be considered, especially in institutional settings where third parties frequently hold substantial amounts in custody.

The private key was first frequently kept as a paper wallet; it was physically written on a piece of paper held securely. Professional custody solutions for various use cases have emerged due to the growing adoption of digital assets. Institutional custody systems provide integrated OCDD checks, customer-specific attributed wallets (also known as "segregated wallets"), or the division of the private key into multiple components (also known as "multi-signature") depending on customer requirements or operational factors. Additionally, they provide connections to conventional systems, insurance protection, or third-party certification.

Although the infrastructure and technology are now accessible, integrating them into financial institutions' legacy systems is still difficult. Examples include varying trading hours in the core banking system (CBS), constantly open trading platforms for digital assets (including both central cryptocurrency exchanges and DEX), or the reconciliation of booked holdings between the core banking system and the blockchain.

Operational challenges include, in particular, the divergent trading hours between the 24/7 crypto exchanges and the posting options in the primary banking system. Often, end-of-day processing prevents the CBS from being accessible for a specific period, which prevents bookings in the core banking system from being feasible around the clock.

The same is true for trading divisions, which follow standard securities sector trading hours and are typically unstaffed on weekends and public holidays. Therefore, investors cannot respond to market changes, profit from them, or lower their own risk during these periods.

Regulation

The Token and Trustworthy Technology Service Providers Act (TVTG) in Liechtenstein, register securities in Switzerland, an expansion of the Travel Rule's applicability to digital assets, and other legislative changes centered on distributed ledger technology are just a few examples of the proliferation of laws governing digital assets in recent years.

Additional regulations, such as the EU's Markets in Crypto Assets, are expected to be implemented (MiCA; framework for the overall regulation of DLT-based assets such as stablecoins or digital assets as well as related services such as the custody of private keys). Infrequently, although to a different degree than "traditional" digital assets like Bitcoin, the DeFi industry is also impacted.

The relatively new asset class of digital assets is frequently subjected to standard regulatory principles from established businesses. These are operationally easier to execute for Bitcoin than for DeFi apps for a financial institution that provides access to digital assets (also known as a "Virtual Asset Service Provider" or "VASP").

This is primarily because DeFi applications based on smart contracts are decentralized. Trading in DeFi via decentralized exchanges is automated and powered by smart contracts, unlike trading in digital assets like Bitcoin or Ethereum on more centralized crypto exchanges. In this regard, the central counterparty can only be effectively addressed through regulation (e.g., people in charge of running the crypto exchange, whether it is decentralized).

Evaluating the counterparty and, eventually, the so-called beneficial owner (BO) in DeFi is crucial. It is nearly hard to identify the "effective" counterparty in current DeFi implementations because of the peer-to-peer nature of a smart intermediary contract, which is also not a formal legal organization.

Financial institutions are typically obliged to confirm a transaction's recipient(s) before executing it or to only transact with approved counterparties, for instance, to comply with sanctions restrictions or stop violations of money laundering legislation.

The blockchain industry has recently increased, particularly in overcoming obstacles and developing new business models. To illustrate the first methods that give regulated institutions access to decentralized finance, we will present a few use scenarios in the following paragraphs.

Selected Use Cases Access Whitelisting for DeFi

Identified trading partners can now access a DeFi loan pool thanks to the creation of Aave Arc by US-based institutional custody solutions company Fireblocks and lending protocol Aave. The technical framework for access, digital asset custody, and trading party onboarding is provided by Fireblocks. Before being granted access to the loan pool, Fireblocks customers who want to use this service must undergo a know-your-client procedure. This procedure is also referred to as "whitelisting," which can be compared to a guest list that complies with regulations. Aave Arc contributes technology and the DeFi application to this procedure.

Aave Arc's whitelisted users have access to the same features as the open Aave DeFi application. They can take on the roles of lender, borrower, or liquidator (protecting against loan failure by securing capital repayment).

Aave Arc provides solutions to the following problems for financial institutions using DeFi: The infrastructure meets institutional requirements in terms of technology (e.g., certification of the infrastructure and processes from an outside, impartial source or the development of suitable interfaces to integrate with preexisting internal IT framework) or integration depth into existing systems.

One hand knows who their lending pool counterparty is. Therefore, it is essential to consider whether or not this is a genuine decentralized solution, how returns will react in response to risk, and how this whitelisting can affect liquidity.

. . .

Securitization of Liquidity Provider Tokens (LPT)

New LPT has been securitized by the Swiss bank Sygnum to access DeFi assets differently. This resolves several issues from the investor's standpoint; for instance, the banking and securities house license guarantees that pertinent regulations are followed. The DeFi tokens' securitization boosts the product's accessibility by relying on an established, reputable, and extensively utilized infrastructure (including ISIN).

As the DeFi tokens' custodian, Sygnum handles all blockchain-related transactions, substantially lowering the operational risk and investor effort. However, due to LPT being securitized, it is not viable to take part in the underlying business models of DeFi applications like yield farming or liquidity mining.

With this new DeFi product, Sygnum Bank can diversify its portfolio of investments and establish itself as a leader in the controlled management of DeFi tokens..

Using a DeFi Application to increase the size of your own business

In April 2022, the Swiss broker Bitcoin Suisse introduced a product that enables a limited number of customers to get blockchain-based loans through the DeFi application Liquity[16]. Customers of Bitcoin Suisse can deposit Ethereum that the broker is holding in the Liquidity smart contract in exchange for the token LUSD, a stablecoin pegged to the dollar. The token can then be converted into a legitimate currency, like CHF.

Using a smart contract; the LUSD is automatically minted without needing an intermediary. Apart from the blockchain transaction fees, the one-time startup price for using the smart contract, and the minting fee for the LUSD, there are no additional costs for investors.

For the investor, the broker handles the management of the blockchain-based digital assets, the transaction to the smart contract, and any desired LUSD exchange. In reality, the broker provides its clients with the option of using the digital assets under their custody as collateral for liquidity, just like a traditional Lombard loan.

Summary and prognosis

Financial institutions with a primary digital asset offering have various chances to enhance their service offerings thanks to decentralized finance, giving them a solid foundation to pursue future revenue streams from digital assets and evolving business models. Financial institutions face difficulties linking the necessary infrastructure to current systems and assuring counterparty verification, but these problems still need to be fully resolved through individual solutions.

The acceptance of DeFi coins and DeFi applications by financial institutions present the DeFi sector with a wonderful chance to increase the number of users, gain access to fresh liquidity, and create a central point of contact for traditional investor groups. The chosen use examples show how authorized financial institutions and blockchain businesses can start taking advantage of DeFi prospects and contributing to the growth of this subset of digital assets.

By employing a systematic methodology to evaluate the effects of DeFi on its business model and challenge its view of what it means to be an intermediary, any financial institution may immediately start to confront the greatest problem. Financial institutions, in particular, need to reevaluate their self-perception as gatekeepers and mediators in the conventional financial world and shift their focus toward becoming partners in their clients' cooperative endeavors. In the future, a bank might, for instance, store a portion of a customer's private key and apply its skills as a reliable and secure custodian of valuables to the context of digital assets.

Why decentralized finance is a technological leapfrog for the 1.1 billion unbanked people

The mobile phone, whose acceptance allowed even the most deprived places to forgo altogether the need to install traditional telecommunications infrastructures like wire networks and landline capabilities, is the technology that best epitomizes the "leapfrog technology" phenomenon.

Today, 83.4% of people worldwide are thought to own mobile phones. In reality, 1.1 billion of the 1.7 billion unbanked adults (22% of the adult population) are said to have access to a mobile phone. These people's initial interactions with financial services will probably be through decentralized infrastructure.

Similar to how smartphones have the potential to be a leapfrog technology, decentralized finance technology might give previously unbanked people access to previously unavailable digital services and assets.

Who are the unbanked?

People with no account with any financial service provider are referred to as the unbanked. Peer-to-peer (P2P) microlending, community savings clubs, and other informal social and community funding methods predating the contemporary banking system need to be recognized by this definition.

According to estimates, the "informal economy" accounts for up to 35% of all economic activity in developing countries. This translates to trillions of dollars of "informal economic activity" that runs parallel to official financial services. The majority of unbanked people reside in developing nations with young populations.

DeFi infrastructure disintermediates banks by providing "accounts," savings and loans, payments, and investing in a model based on technology and P2P. Financial instruments are software, capital is crowdfunded, and community-sourced and the game's rules are open and based on code.

As a result, a financial system that is borderless, open, public, transparent, and censorship-resistant is created. And one that everyone in the world may access with just a smartphone and an internet connection.

Decentralized finance has grown to be a $1 billion sector in less than five years, with a market cap of more than $180 billion. DeFi subscribers have increased from 91,000 in January 2020 to almost five million.

Let's be clear: Up to this point, DeFi's volume and activity have only focused on crypto-financial applications, which are popular among the unkindly referred-to "degenerates" crowd.

The unbanked population has not yet fully embraced decentralized finance, nor has it been created with them in mind. However, the figures on cryptocurrency acceptance compel us to keep a careful eye on DeFi adoption rates.

Developing nations lead in cryptocurrency adoption

Except for the United States, emerging nations lead developed nations in adopting, mining, and trading cryptocurrencies. Four of the seven countries with the greatest percentage of unbanked adults also happen to be the countries with the highest rate of cryptocurrency adoption. Many crypto-hungry countries have a high percentage of unbanked citizens (China, India, Pakistan, Nigeria).

Globally, unbanked and underbanked communities have relatively greater adoption rates of cryptocurrency ownership than those fully banked, especially in industrialized economies with established financial services industries like the US.

The current unbanked will never become "banked," instead moving right into decentralized financial services. This forecast is supported by three main factors, specifically:

The decentralized financial system's transparent, unrestricted nature where anyone can build a blockchain wallet, which is essential for anyone with a mobile device and internet connectivity to use DeFi rails to access blockchain-native financial services and the world's capital markets.

As an "account," the blockchain-based digital wallet can send, receive, store, and invest digital assets. This is a portal for obtaining foreign currency, transacting it, and gaining access to international capital markets.

Unsurprisingly, huge segments want to receive payments in digital currencies and transfer wealth into decentralized digital currencies like bitcoin and Ethereum in economies like Argentina, Venezuela, and Nigeria. Cryptocurrencies are the world's most widely held asset type due to their permissionless nature.

DeFi enhances the P2P community financial models now in use.

The current informal, social, and financial infrastructure can be improved via decentralized finance innovations on community-based financial structures. These innovations offer safer, more practical, and more dependable solutions.

For those who cannot on-ramp via centralized financial institutions, the P2P exchange is already pushing cryptocurrency adoption in emerging nations. Savings and loan arrangements based on DeFi are next. Savings groups are a popular community-based strategy for setting aside funds and granting loans to help community members.

A DeFi-based strategy offers the following advantages: while automating payments and withdrawals ensures fairness and transparency for all members, digital payments are safer, easier to trace, and less error-prone than physical cash and manual ledger keeping.

Unlike cash, digital community funds could be invested smoothly, and geographical restrictions on savings communities were no longer necessary. The traceable, auditable credit records produced by this on-chain data can be a gateway to more considerable sums of finance from external borrowers.

The advantages of universal basic income in crypto

The growing interest in cryptocurrency-based universal basic income is proof of the ever-increasing understanding that decentralized finance offers effective means for funding and distributing capital over time. Blockchain enables efficient direct money distribution to individuals at scale.

These revolutionary concepts are becoming more widely accepted as a practical business model for humanity, with more than one billion people surviving on less than $1.90 daily. Numerous diverse strategies have recently progressed to new levels of feasibility.

GoodDollar and Impact Market have onboarded more than 500,000 users to distributed crypto UBI and non-custodial wallets, mostly from nations like Nigeria, India, and Indonesia. The recipients have utilized the money to support necessities, engage in peer-to-peer trading, and research DeFi tools like savings groups.

These initiatives integrate the underbanked with decentralized finance assets and infrastructure, and they have the potential to spread quickly.

The adoption of decentralized finance has difficulties.

It is impossible to overestimate the dangers and difficulties of adopting decentralized finance. Financial literacy is a good start, but more is needed since DeFi products and assets still need to be created to support vulnerable populations despite the apparent simplicity of storing cryptocurrency in a digital wallet. Basic literacy is still an issue, and 37% of the world's population still lacks widespread and affordable Web access, which is necessary for development.

Even the most developed cryptocurrencies pose a serious threat to those living paycheck to paycheck due to their extreme volatility, which can potentially lose 72% of their value in a year. The lack of consumer protection and unstable markets will always threaten the adoption of DeFi in the absence of defined regulations and boundaries, and Mega-trends are only one factor in adoption.

Leapfrogging to DeFi has effects beyond just cutting out the middleman. It makes it possible for more people to have open access to and participate in the new digital economy. Additionally, it may increase access to well-known financial concepts and products while empowering previously underserved areas to engage in capital building.

The unbanked may readily embrace and participate in a truly decentralized global economy because of the foundations that decentralized finance has established.

Decentralized Finance: Four Issues to Take into Account

What would the world be like without banks? Decentralized finance, a $77 billion business hailed as a more effective substitute for traditional banking, is founded on this idea.

In a DeFi future, cryptocurrency-backed transactions are automatically carried out, and blockchain-based smart contracts allow for direct commerce between individuals without the interference of central banks or any institutions.

The distributed ledger technology at the core of cryptocurrencies and DeFi, in the words of MIT Sloan finance professor and cryptocurrency researcher Antoinette Schoar, co-director of the Corporate Finance program at the National Bureau of Economic Research, "is a core innovation that can potentially change the architecture of our existing financial infrastructure."

The financial system has historically relied heavily on intermediaries, including commercial and investment banks, stockbrokers, and pooled investment funds. Schoar stated that the "new financial infrastructure offers to do away with the intermediaries and institutions and replace them with a network of decentralized participants on the blockchain, notably in DeFi."

Cryptocurrency supporters praise decentralized finance as a means of democratizing finance. Public blockchains and open-source software, instead of traditional financial institutions and banking fees, would allow virtually anybody with an Internet connection to participate for free, according to proponents.

Schoar and co-author Igor Makarov of the London School of Economics examined these and other assertions in a new working paper titled "Cryptocurrencies and Decentralized Finance."

DeFi, according to the authors, has the potential to transform the financial industry, but there are still many issues that need to be resolved first, such as regulation and transparency.

DeFi lacks consumer protections which is present in traditional finance and is a magnet for fraud and money laundering because it is mostly unregulated. According to statistics from the blockchain analytics company Elliptic, more than $10 billion was lost in 2021 due to DeFi frauds.

DeFi nevertheless presents a lot of potential and possibility. Here are four key findings from the study:

1. DeFi isn't an even playing field

Schoar argued that it is "very foolish to expect" that DeFi will instantly level the playing field despite its claim to democratize access. According to her, economies of scale and scope and significant network externalities are naturally vulnerable to financial markets, and even when there is free market access, these dynamics pressure concentrations.

For instance, traders would always want to execute their order on the deepest and most liquid exchange, given the significance of liquidity for exchanges. However, this allows the exchange to impose high costs. "DeFi marketplaces begin to exhibit the same pattern. High fees are charged by dominating exchanges, and they work to maintain that position.

As evidenced by the conflict between Uniswap and Sushi-Swap, major exchanges, even in the DeFi sector, are attempting to restrict access to their trade secrets to increase the difficulty of competition. She claimed that if you have dominant exchanges, it will be challenging for others to overtake them, even if they can enter quickly.

2. It takes more work to collect taxes

Even for the well-intentioned, reporting transactions using digital currency is difficult given that DeFi is primarily based on permissionless and pseudonymous blockchains, according to researchers. In fact, according to a Barclays estimate, the IRS may be losing out on $50 billion in unpaid crypto taxes each year because it's challenging to track down these transactions and remit taxes.

"It's tough to impose taxes in the DeFi world. No intermediaries exist that have the infrastructure to collect taxes, confirm your identity, and then send the IRS a 1088 tax form or a capital gains notification," according to Schoar. Even for those who desire to act morally, it is highly inconvenient.

According to Schoar, software that can determine a person's crypto tax may exist in the future, and this may aid the ability to self-report taxes. However, it's simple for people to avoid paying taxes on cryptocurrency, "providing one segment of the financial system a tremendous subsidy over the traditional financial sector where we do collect taxes," as the author puts it.

3. Governance issues plague the sector

DeFi governance, in contrast to traditional finance, is carried out by decentralized autonomous groups. Similar to a crypto co-op, a DAO distributes decision-making authority among all interested parties by allowing a community of users to vote on ideas using cryptocurrency tokens.

That configuration, however, is not immune to the same governance issues that have dogged the crypto industry more broadly. For instance, the first-ever DAO, dubbed The DAO, garnered more than $150 million but eventually had to be delisted due to severe governance issues.

Additionally, the authors claimed that given the blockchain's anonymity. It would be challenging to execute fines if significant stakeholder investors (also known as "block-holders") obtained enough authority to push their views on the system.

About the area outside of the blockchain, the authors write, "There has been little evidence so far to imply that the crypto sector can successfully tackle governance challenges without relying on some off-chain methods."

They go on to state that "strong governance mechanisms will certainly need the backing of external regulation" given that "governance concerns of blockchain platforms and traditional financial institutions are not significantly different."

4. There could be better global regulatory coordination

International laws governing cryptocurrency and DeFi vary, but according to Schoar, more worldwide regulatory coordination would help reduce fraud. "There are different regulatory approaches in Europe and the US, and Europe is further ahead than the US. "The fact that so many agencies in the United States could interact with cryptocurrencies means these agencies will need to work together to find a solution.

There are ways to control the DeFi system. According to Schoar, that would maintain the majority of the benefits of blockchain design while promoting responsibility and legal compliance. For instance, blockchain validators could be obliged to confirm that a specific address belongs to a certified company before processing any transactions involving certified addresses.

Schoar favored building an infrastructure that enables cooperation between decentralized entities and regulators. That may guarantee that only players who abide by Know Your Client, anti-money laundering, and anti-terrorism restrictions can put transactions on the blockchain.

This way, as she explains, "We could ensure that the blockchain ecosystem complies with these fundamental requirements, at least for most inhabitants of nations like the US or Europe that agree on these norms. If we work well together, we can keep most of that architecture's benefits while safeguarding our economy against criminal conduct, such as tax evasion."

The future of DeFi

While advancements in DeFi and crypto might have advantages in the future, such as the potential to lower transaction costs, it's crucial to remember that they still need to demonstrate their value, according to Schoar. Given that DeFi blockchains are anonymous, it may lead to new issues like tax evasion if there needs to be more oversight.

To many, DeFi represents a brave new world that vastly improves conventional finance's efficiency. However, Schoar claimed that both universes suffer from the same economic problem regarding intermediaries since "financial markets are particularly prone to becoming monopolized without any intervention."

The authors wrote that the stability of the American and other developed economies ultimately depends on how this [DeFi] system develops in terms of technology and legislation.

Key features in this chapter

- Campbell Harvey argued that the age of centralized finance may be ending and the age of decentralized finance may be just getting started at the Alpha Summit GLOBAL by CFA Institute last month.
- Professional custody solutions for various use cases have emerged due to the growing adoption of digital assets.
- Examples include varying trading hours in the core banking system (CBS), constantly open trading platforms for digital assets (including both central cryptocurrency exchanges and DEX), or the reconciliation of booked holdings between the core banking system and the blockchain.
- The relatively new asset class of digital assets is frequently subjected to standard regulatory principles from established businesses.
- Identified trading partners can now access a DeFi loan pool thanks to the creation of Aave Arc by US-based institutional custody solutions company Fireblocks and lending protocol Aave.
- Similar to how smartphones have the potential to be a leapfrog technology, decentralized finance technology might give previously unbanked people access to previously unavailable digital services and assets.
- International laws governing cryptocurrency and DeFi vary, but according to Schoar, more worldwide regulatory coordination would help reduce fraud.
- With more resources and financial protocols, building a composable centralized infrastructure is

conceivable, but given the difficulties in governing permissioned ledgers, this would be dangerous.

- Privacy concerns may be raised by the blockchain's openness and decentralized approach to block formation.

6

HOW TO INVEST IN DEFI?

DeFi has developed over the previous few years into a fully-fledged alternative financial system with over $250 billion in value at its most recent peak in November 2021. However, this phrase still needs clarification by excessive intricacy. This section explains how to invest in DeFi, outlines several prospects, and provides a straightforward step-by-step tutorial. It goes beyond the jargon.

Why is DeFi so well-liked right now?

The development of blockchain technologies and the acceptance of cryptocurrencies facilitated the emergence of the alternative financial system. DeFi enables anyone to do financial transactions more quickly, affordably, and independently.

Lending, borrowing, trading, and more can be done through open-source protocols on a decentralized financial network without waiting for authorization from a bank or another entity. You and the smart contract are the only two parties involved in processing your request; there are no back offices or levels of management.

The essential requirement for using DeFi is a non-custodial cryptocurrency wallet. You can navigate the DeFi world with a clever Web3 wallet like Zerion, which tracks all of your tokens across more than ten networks.

Let's now explore decentralized finance investment strategies.

Investment options for DeFi

First of all, keep in mind that all investments involve risk. DeFi is on the higher end of the risk range, similar to the rest of the crypto market. Even if something seems risk-free, there may be dangers that you are unaware of. Any guarantees of returns or profits ought to be taken seriously. Let's now examine the various chances you have to invest in DeFi.

Asset DeFi trading

The most direct route to exposure to decentralized finance is through direct investment in DeFi assets. The basic concept is to buy and trade DeFi coins and tokens. Of course, it is far more challenging to turn a profit that way. Although many people mistakenly think of tokens and coins as having the same function, they differ slightly.

DeFi tokens are resources linked to particular DeFi protocols. Tokens are utilized differently by each protocol. Some tokens give their owners voting privileges, and others might be staked to generate income. Finally, specific tokens are periodically "burned" (i.e., destroyed), which lowers the overall supply and functions similarly to a share buyback on the stock market.

DeFi tokens include, for instance:

- UNI, the largest decentralized exchange's governance token from Uniswap;
- MAKER, the MakerDAO governance token, which powers the DAI stablecoin system;
- AAVE, the cryptocurrency of Aave, the biggest platform for lending and borrowing;
- SNX, the token used to produce synthetic assets through the Synthetix system.

To interact with decentralized finance, you must pay gas fees for each network transaction. The blockchain's native currency is used to pay the fees: ETH for Ethereum, MATIC for Polygon, etc.

Purchasing the underlying currencies may be the simplest method to invest in decentralized finance without spending much time learning about DeFi protocols.

In DeFi, some examples of coins used to pay for gas include:

- ETH for use on Ethereum's main network;
- MATIC for the network using Polygon Proof of Stake;
- AVAX for Avalanche, an Ethereum Layer-1 substitute;
- FTM for Fantom, the Layer-1 network with a DeFi focus.

These coins can be kept in your wallet (holding) or used in different DeFi protocols to generate a yield, such as through staking.

DeFi staking

DeFi staking is a low-risk approach to generating a passive income. DeFi assets are staked to be locked in a smart contract and receive a payout. The same tokens are used by numerous DeFi protocols to reward their users.

Example: betting on optimism with SNX:

1. To avoid paying high gas prices on Ethereum, purchase SNX tokens on the Optimism network.
2. Go to https://staking.synthetix.io/
3. Connect your wallet
4. Stake your SNX to generate sUSD; you will receive stake rewards in both sUSD and SNX.

Staking SNX

Staking rewards typically have a set, variable, or annual percentage yield (APY). Therefore, you receive greater DeFi rewards if you invest more tokens. High-staking APY, however, could be misleading. If a DeFi token offered 100% APY but crashed by 90%, the outcome might not be that appealing.

DeFi yield farming

Staking has been upgraded to yield farming. The phrase is derived from how farmers can increase their income by switching from one crop to another and was first used as a meme. Similar to DeFi, yield farming involves switching between various farms.

With DeFi yield farming, you could perform some action for the DeFi protocol, obtain another token for that action, and then stake that token instead of staking a single asset (like SNX). An illustration might make this concept clearer.

An illustration would be the Aurora network's Trisolaris yield farming tokens.

1. Provide liquidity for a pool of farm rewards on the Trisolaris exchange in exchange for the LP token.
2. Put that LP token on the farm as a stake.
3. receive farm rewards (TRI and other tokens).
4. To increase your benefits, stake your TRI tokens.

Farms on Trisolaris

There are numerous varieties of yield farms, such as:

- Provider of Liquidity Depositing coins on a decentralized exchange (DEX) will give traders access to liquidity. The native tokens of the DEX, and any farmed tokens, will be earned in addition to the trading fee from trade traders make.
- Lending. Using smart contracts, token owners lend digital assets to other users and make money from the interest on the loans. Additionally, the network has a token it can use to reward lenders.
- Borrowing. Pledge one token as collateral to borrow another currency and pay the interest. The benefits to the borrowers frequently outweigh the interest they pay. Don't worry if this needs to be clarified. You don't have to handle everything by yourself. Many automated platforms have been developed to make yield farming easier for frequent users:
- Yearn.finance
- Harvest.finance
- Beefy.finance

DeFi lending

Lending is a different way to diversify your DeFi investment portfolio. Most lending methods rely on loans with collateral:

- Lenders can lend other people money in cryptocurrency.
- Borrowers can borrow another asset while locking up some assets as collateral. For instance, a borrower might borrow USDT while locking up ETH as security.

The algorithm used by lending procedures often bases interest rates on the supply and demand for loans. As a result, there will be a higher interest rate if there is a great demand. This is frequently the case on other Layer-1 networks, such as Aave's Avalanche markets, which also offer extra benefits in the form of AVAX (do you notice the red asterisks on the screen below?).

The earliest and most well-known venues for borrowing and lending:

- Aave
- Compound

DeFi indexes

Investing in a DeFi index is a convenient way to join Decentralized Finance and diversify your cryptocurrency portfolio. DeFi indices invest in various assets by predetermined principles, much like ETFs in conventional finance. For instance, this is what the Phuture DeFi Index contains:

Underlying tokens of Phuture DeFi Index

The market cap and price performance are the two most crucial elements to take into account when choosing an index. Although historical results do not guarantee future results, they demonstrate the index's volatility and price changes under various market conditions. The market cap, meanwhile, reveals how well-liked the index is. DeFi indexes with higher market capitalization should be more reliable (although there are no guarantees).

Some of the most widely used DeFi indices:

- Phuture DeFi Index
- DeFi Pulse Index
- Metaverse Index
- Bankless BED Index

How can I purchase DeFi tokens?

You need to know where to get DeFi tokens now that you know your DeFi investment options. Different centralized exchanges (CEXes) provide simple interfaces that make selling and purchasing DeFi cryptocurrency simple and easy onboarding from fiat (i.e., paying using bank cards). Popular exchanges with lots of DeFi tokens include:

- Binance
- Coinbase
- Kraken

However, many recent DeFi currencies are frequently exclusively offered through decentralized exchanges (DEXes). It would help if you had a Zerion Wallet or another non-custodial cryptocurrency wallet to purchase tokens on these exchanges. The largest DEXes include:

- Uniswap
- SushiSwap
- PancakeSwap

Prices frequently range across several decentralized exchanges. By automatically searching all DEXes, Zerion's trading aggregation can help you locate the best price and ensure you purchase DeFi tokens at the lowest possible cost. Zerion will identify the appropriate DEX for you after you link your wallet. Pick the token you want to buy and the asset you want to use to pay for it.

A step-by-step approach to investing in DeFi

Following your decision to invest in DeFi, you must take the actions on this checklist:

Step 1. Create a wallet: A non-custodial wallet, such as Zerion Wallet, is recommended for staking and lending with DeFi.

The Zerion Wallet is perfect for DeFi:

- Keep tabs on all DeFi assets, including staked tokens, liquidity pools, farms, and loans.
- Discover the top swaps on DEXes.
- Quickly choose between more than 10 Layer-1 and Layer-2 networks.

Step 2. Choose your blockchain network: Once your crypto wallet is complete, choose the main DeFi network and start investing. Ethereum is still the most often used blockchain when talking about DeFi. However, its high gas prices can make it prohibitively expensive when first getting started. On some days, the cost of a simple transaction can exceed $10, and the cost of a more complex operation, such as lending tokens, can reach $100. Ethereum's Layer-2 scaling solutions and other Layer-1 networks have transaction prices below $1.

The following are the popular networks that Zerion Wallet supports:

- Arbitrum
- Avalanche
- Aurora
- Fantom
- Arbitrum

Step 3. Fund your wallet: Buy the platform-specific tokens (FTM for Fantom, ETH for Ethereum, etc.) from a cryptocurrency exchange. These digital currencies are available for purchase through Zerion Wallet's on-ramp or one of the controlled exchanges.

Step 4. Acquire your DeFi coins: It would help to buy the proper DeFi coins or tokens once you've decided on the DeFi protocol you want to invest in. Token purchases can be made directly in Zerion Wallet, automatically locating the best price for you or on any decentralized exchanges.

. . .

Step 5. Stake, lend, and use DeFi protocols: DeFi enables you to keep control of your assets. We've discussed how you can lend, stake, or provide liquidity with your tokens to get paid. The "Explore" tool in Zerion that displays some of the options you have in DeFi is the simplest method to test this out.

Step 6. Choose a liquidity pool: Another option to diversify your DeFi holdings would be to invest in liquidity pools.

The Pools page in Zerion makes it incredibly simple to sign up for some of the most well-liked liquidity pools with only a few taps.

One of the rapidly expanding investment trends in cryptocurrency is DeFi. However, there are some hazards, just like with any other investment. It's crucial to start small, observe how DeFi investing functions, and conduct your study before spending a hefty sum.

The Best Way io Invest in DeFi Projects

With a focus on decentralized access to financial services, DeFi has recently been one of the hottest issues. Imagine a worldwide network of financial services without a single bank or insurer. For specific reasons, more and more people are becoming interested in investing in DeFi cryptocurrency. You must pick the best DeFi crypto coins with a high likelihood of success. However, it's crucial to remember that investing in DeFi carries several dangers, notably volatility.

On the other side, there is little you can do to stop people from becoming curious about how to invest in DeFi projects, mainly as they grow in popularity. The breadth of DeFi will be briefly discussed in the following section where the safety issues regarding DeFi investments will be discussed. The topic of investing in DeFi projects and some well-known DeFi crypto coins to explore will also be covered.

Summary of DeFi

It's crucial to comprehend the fundamentals of DeFi and the scope of the technology before beginning your search for the finest DeFi cryptocurrency to buy in 2023. How relevant is decentralized finance? Does it merit a potential investor's attention?

Currently, assets worth nearly $70 million are locked in DeFi protocols worldwide. It is logical to assume that the DeFi sector can offer profitable investment prospects. Beginners, however, needed help comprehending how decentralized financial services access can provide any investing chance.

Investment potential in DeFi

Consider the DeFi definition once more, and you will see how Ethereum's programmability characteristic makes it possible to create smart contracts. Anyone with a cryptocurrency wallet can utilize the DeFi program, and smart contracts describe the specific duties of a DeFi protocol. The ambiguity around DeFi investment funds would also highlight the distinctions between DeFi and conventional finance.

Here, we highlight the critical value advantages DeFi provides over conventional finance while pointing out the potential for investment in DeFi. Users can borrow and lend money, carry out transactions like payments, and make returns on their investments based on arbitrage and speculation, just as in traditional finance. By giving people more control, DeFi improves the financial services industry.

DeFi platforms allow users to transact within financial services without having their data or assets controlled by a centralized middleman. On DeFi platforms, investors can lend their assets in exchange for interest and extra benefits like the native DeFi crypto tokens. Nevertheless, knowing the dangers of investing in DeFi ventures is also critical.

Is DeFi Good to invest in?

The safety of DeFi is the obvious concern on everyone's mind right now. How can you select the best investment when dealing with DeFi for the first time? The benefits of user anonymity and promises of increased effectiveness come first. Potentially flexible and incredibly attractive returns are advantages of investing in DeFi. It's crucial to remember that DeFi has its hazards, with regulatory issues being one of the most prominent. Defi's new nature also suggests that it could come with risks you might never have foreseen.

On the other side of the coin, responses to the question "Is DeFi Good to Invest In?" would also highlight dangers because of weaknesses in the smart contract code. Investors may also be exposed to the risks of cryptocurrency frauds like rug pulls. It's also vital to remember that, like traditional investments, DeFi investments have a risk appetite. The main issue with DeFi investments is the purported "self-governance and decentralization." The conventional functions played by banks are typically replaced by smaller groups of stakeholders in DeFi protocols, eliminating the decentralization aspect.

However, it's also crucial to remember that DeFi protocols lack shock absorbers. As a result, if there are any tragic accidents without any safety measures or insurance, you will lose everything. DeFi investment money is always in danger because there is no safety net. Investment in appropriate research, however, can still open up the possibility of funding

DeFi projects. By evaluating several DeFi protocol-related parameters, you can gauge the level of risk you are willing to take on for a particular investment inside DeFi.

Where can I invest in DeFi Projects?

Any advice on investing in DeFi cryptocurrency would emphasize how simple it is to use DeFi programs. DeFi protocols can be immediately interacted with, and you can study the new market. Users of DeFi must gain a thorough understanding of cryptocurrency as well as how DeFi protocols operate.

You can quickly learn more about DeFi protocols with the fundamental procedures, such as linking your cryptocurrency wallet to a DeFi application. The cryptocurrency wallet, Metamask, accessible as a browser extension, is one of the best wallets for DeFi applications. You can use the services of many DeFi programs after adding the necessary quantity of crypto tokens, such as ETH, to your crypto wallet.

The methods utilized for investing your assets in DeFi protocols will undoubtedly be highlighted in the talks about choosing the finest DeFi investment. Here is a list of the top suggestions for funding DeFi projects.

- **Staking**: Staking is a common strategy for earning DeFi income without actively doing anything. DeFi users can generate interest on deposited tokens and lock their tokens in a protocol for a set amount of time. Users have a choice between two different approaches to staking. In the first approach, selecting a Proof of Stake blockchains like Cardano or Solana would be advised. The tokens can then be locked within the relevant blockchain while also providing flexibility for transaction verification. On the other hand, leveraging external staking platforms is a key component of solving the question of "how to invest in DeFi projects" with staking. The protocol's smart contract allows users to deposit their tokens, which can then be used to fund liquidity pools and loans. One of the well-known examples of a third-party staking platform that enables users to stake the platform's native coin for a longer period is DeFi Swap.

- **Interest in Savings Accounts:** Yes, you can open a crypto savings account and test your investment potential in DeFi initiatives. You can use crypto tokens collecting dust in your wallet as savings in DeFi accounts. Depending upon the protocol, DeFi accounts may provide a higher yield than regular cash deposits. Additionally, some DeFi protocols enable higher rates when staking local tokens. One of the better DeFi investment cases in a savings account would be Aqru, which offers cryptocurrency interest accounts. Additionally, it has given customers flexibility by preventing restrictions from locking up their funds and enabling withdrawal anytime.

- **Yield farming:** The most popular option for investing in DeFi cryptocurrency would be yield farming. Contrary to popular belief, yield farming shares many characteristics with staking in that it involves lending cryptocurrency or DeFi tokens to a decentralized exchange or application. In this scenario, you would act as a liquidity provider for the lending/borrowing application or the exchange. As a liquidity provider, you may guarantee that buyers and sellers can conduct transactions on a DeFi marketplace without relying on intermediaries. A portion of the rewards for the transaction fees can be earned by investors who contribute their assets to certain liquidity pools and engage in transactions there.

- **Stablecoins**: One of the toughest problems for investors is the volatility in the DeFi business. Stablecoins, on the other hand, might be a big help in providing the stability you need for passive returns on your DeFi tokens. If you have a specific platform's DeFi crypto tokens, you can convert them into stablecoins and use the savings account strategy. With stablecoins, you must consider the hazards as well. To explore the possibility of larger profits with DeFi savings accounts, you should also try reputable stablecoins like USD Coin or DAI

- **Integration of NFTs and DeFi**: The merging of NFTs and DeFi is a different suggestion for "how to invest in DeFi initiatives." You can fully control your DeFi wallets by incorporating NFTs. Lucky Block is a promising illustration of using DeFi to invest in NFTs. Through the primary listing, the gaming platform has successfully developed about 10,000 different NFTs. Investments in NFTs through DeFi protocols can help investors achieve their goals as the popularity of NFTs rises

Best DeFi Coins to Buy in 2023

The decentralized finance industry has taken off over the last couple of years, making many early investors extremely pleased. It might be challenging to locate the finest Defi cryptos, but it doesn't have to be. In this section, we'll examine 14 of the top Defi coins to purchase, discuss if Defi cryptocurrencies are a decent investment and what exchange may be the best for doing so in 2023.

Top 14 Defi coins to buy in 2023

The top Defi cryptos to buy right now are included in a quick overview below, and more in-depth analyses of each project can be found further down the page. We listed below various top Defi investments to provide aspiring investors with plenty of options. Each of these initiatives has a lot of potential and a solid foundation.

1. FightOut, the best Defi coin to invest in, with up to 50% in purchase bonuses.

The next-generation move-to-earn platform FightOut pays users for finishing workouts and other fitness-related activities. With its innovative ideas and early solid pre-sale success, FightOut has the potential to rank among the top cryptocurrency pre-sale ventures. When the pre-sale is over, the price of FightOut's native token, $FGHT, will have raised 100% to $0.0333 from its current reduced price of $0.0166. Incentives of up to 50% are available to early investors during the inaugural pre-sale round, which is now 50% complete, based on the number of FGHT tokens they purchase and the length of time they choose to lock their tokens.

FightOut has developed fitness software that rewards users for finishing exercises and in-app challenges. The company also has grand aspirations to construct actual, Web3-integrated gyms in strategic global areas. By building a metaverse for its users and using NFT avatars to reflect their digital fitness profiles, FightOut has uniquely gamified fitness.

With FightOut's smart technology that takes into consideration movement, key effort indicators, sleep, and nutrition, the profile is built using soul bound avatars that correlate to and record improvements to match the users' fitness gains. Users may compete with other community members in the project's metaverse to win prizes.

FightOut created REPS, an in-app, off-chain currency, to reward users. REPS are given to users as incentives for doing their daily exercises and fitness-related motions. Additionally, players can utilize the in-app cash to purchase goods from the FightOut store. They may buy membership discounts, merchandise, cosmetic NFTs, and other intriguing goods.

FightOut's whitepaper provides a more in-depth look at the project's features and is available to interested parties. The total native token supply of Fightout ($FGHT) is 10 billion, of which 90% is available for pre-sale purchases, and the remaining 10% is reserved for exchange liquidity.

Buyers may use the $FGHT token to get access to premium leagues and tournaments, unlock additional game modes, and other things. The tokens may also be used to buy more REPS. In this scenario, customers purchasing REPS with $FGHT would get an extra 25% REPS.

Within days of the pre-sale beginning, the project received an outstanding response, raising more than $2 million in less than a week. Investors are invited to join the FightOut Telegram group to remain informed regularly.

2. Popular Defi token to buy in 2023: Dash 2 Trade

The next-best Defi token to buy for 2023 is D2T, the native cryptocurrency of the Dash 2 Trade crypto analytics and intelligence platform. The project, scheduled to launch its initial exchange offering (IEO) on January 23, has announced a four-day overfunding period after enthusiastic investors exceeded the original funding goal.

Along with previously confirmed listings on Uniswap, LBank, BitMart, and Changelly Pro, the project, one of the greatest new cryptocurrencies to invest in 2023, has now revealed it would be listed on Tier 1 controlled exchange Gate.io. D2T, one of the top Defi tokens, may be used to get access to premium features on the Dash 2 Trade interface. Access to on-chain analysis, personal risk profilers, and routine new crypto listing notifications are a few of these tools and use cases.

The Dash Score, a custom cryptocurrency pre-sales evaluation and ranking mechanism, is one key component that has already undergone beta testing and has gotten extremely excellent responses from the community. Other features include trading signals, a learn-to-earn academy for aspiring traders, analytical data to identify emerging trends, and a wide variety of independent professional-grade technical indicators for traders, including moving averages and order book statistics. There are also tools like a backtester and automated trading APIs.

The Dash 2 Trade whitepaper states that this platform will also provide community-wide reward-earning opportunities; D2T token holders may participate in weekly trading contests where the victors can get free Dash 2 Trade tokens. The platform's functionalities are accessible via monthly memberships, which are paid for using D2T.

With 36 million tokens available, D2T tokens are being sold in the overfunding round for $0.0556 each. The chance to participate in the platform's $150,000 D2T contest is another advantage of buying into the pre-sale. To stay up to date on all project updates and breaking news, join the Dash 2 Trade Telegram channel.

3. Newly launched coin offered in exciting pre-sale: C+Charge

C+Charge is a cutting-edge ecosystem that gives carbon credits to electric vehicle (EV) owners who charge their cars. The platform is developing a peer-to-peer platform and mobile that will allow users to pay for charging their vehicles with their native token, $CCHG, and get crucial data that will make EV ownership more practical and efficient.

For stage 1, the pre-sale price for $CCHG is currently $0.013. However, the price of the token increases over the course of the four pre-sale rounds, and by the fourth and final rounds, the price of a $CCHG token has increased by 80% to $0.0235. 40% of the total 1 billion tokens have been set aside by C+Charge for the pre-sale. Individuals who choose not to participate will only have access to 8% of the entire token supply when the currency lists on exchanges.

This ecosystem provides a mobile app with a cryptocurrency wallet that saves $CCHG tokens and tracks the carbon credits that drivers get after charging their cars. Carbon credits are authorizations that enable their owners to lessen their carbon footprint by supporting green initiatives.

Additionally, drivers may use the app to find the closest charging station and see its costs and wait times. The democratization of carbon credits via C+Charge will promote EV adoption. To manage their fleet, charging station operators may also get real-time data from each station and run diagnostics.

Join the Telegram channel and read the whitepaper to learn more about $CCHG and C+Charge. Because just 8% of the $FGHT tokens are designated for exchange liquidity, now is the ideal moment to purchase them.

4. Tamadoge - best Defi meme token to buy in 2023

This new meme currency borrows elements from play-to-earn (P2E) games to provide a unique and captivating experience unmatched by any other. The project had a fantastic debut in late 2022, increasing by around 2,000% from the presale price and solidifying its place among the top 10 meme coins.

Despite a fall in price within the overall bear market, TAMA remains one of the most popular cryptocurrencies and among the finest Defi coins. The project revolves around a Metaverse world where users may amass, train, and engage in combat with Tamadoge dogs built on NFT. By purchasing things from the in-game shop, users may enhance their pets and get Dogepoints, which improves their leaderboard standing and increases their portion of the monthly award pool.

We need to know how far TAMA may climb when the market rebounds, given that Tamadoge is already making waves in the sector and that the price of TAMA is likely to surge once the 5% burn mechanism on income earned from the in-game shop kicks in. In contrast to other meme projects, TAMA offers enormous usefulness thanks to its play-to-earn game, two arcade-style mini-games, and future augmented reality app - in addition to its limited token supply (2 billion) and deflationary process.

Join the Tamadoge Telegram group now to learn more about the project and to get updates on any upcoming advancements or listing announcements.

5. Battle Infinity: strong P2E and Defi ecosystems

A diversified Defi ecosystem called Battle Infinity (IBAT) comprises several fascinating features aimed at helping crypto fans of all sizes and shapes. Battle Infinity created a significant sensation when it joined the cryptocurrency market, similar to Tamadoge.

The IBAT token has grown steadily and shows no signs of slowing down; it has recently also become a staking asset with high APY. The IBAT token went from selling out its pre-sale 65 days before schedule to delivering early investors 4x profits upon its PancakeSwap listing.

The IBAT ecosystem includes:

- A decentralized exchange (DEX).
- A staking platform (scheduled to open on September 24).
- A fantasy sports league.
- An NFT marketplace.
- Several tokenized P2E crypto games.
- Even a Metaverse arena where users may engage in advertising and social interaction.

With such a broad feature set, Battle Infinity appears ready to take off when the platform's key features start to roll out. In light of this, getting some of the finest Defi tokens could be wise before demand increases prices. Sign up for the Battle Infinity Telegram to get notifications of any new updates.

6. Chainlink: Prominent Oracle Solutions Provider

This Defi coin aims to significantly increase the use cases of new crypto projects by transferring off-chain data sources onto the blockchain for usage by other Web3 companies.

Aave, Hedera, and Compound are some of the top Defi crypto projects that use Chainlink as their preferred platform since it was one of the first projects to provide such a service and was adopted by major companies.

It should come as no surprise that LINK has remained one of the market's strongest assets despite the current crypto collapse, given the in-demand Chainlink's services. We'll closely monitor LINK's performance once the next bull run starts because many investors praise it as one of the best long-term cryptocurrency projects. It is currently on the market because the asset exhibits enormous strength whenever the market experiences a slight run-up.

7. XRP: decentralized currency conversion project

Since its debut as a Bitcoin alternative that offers a quick settlement, cheap fees, and sustainability, XRP has been a favored asset among cryptocurrency investors. David Schwartz and Jeb McCaleb are the creators of the asset, and they later established Ripple Labs to develop use cases for XRP.

The main draw of XRP is its extraordinary efficiency. On one of the quickest and least expensive networks available, transactions may be resolved in a matter of seconds and for pennies on the dollar. The recent XRP Ledger (XRPL) launch in 2021 has further broadened the project's use case by enabling the creation of other projects on the network.

XRP is mostly used as a cryptocurrency for transactions. Due to its existing partnerships with well-known international money transfer companies like Swift and MoneyGram, many investors believe the asset is among the top 10 penny cryptocurrency initiatives.

8. Tezos: a competitor to Ethereum that can be upgraded easily

The Defi currency Tezos (XTC) is comparable to a more effective, readily upgradeable Ethereum. The Tezos main net wasn't formally published until much later in 2018, even though the idea was first conceived in 2014. The project uses smart contracts to enable programmers to create apps for the Tezos network. The Tezos network can be quickly updated with minimal downtime, allowing the team to constantly guarantee the network sports the newest technology. The project is continually viewed as a fantastic alternative to Ethereum.

The need for instantly upgradeable blockchains has increased due to the recent Ethereum merger. Many crypto enthusiasts consider Tezos one of the best cryptocurrencies to purchase in 2023 because it provides these features in exceedingly effective packaging.

9. Avalanche: low-cost layer-1 blockchain

Avalanche (AVAX), a brand-new cryptocurrency and very effective layer-1 blockchain, is similar to Tezos. At the height of the "Ethereum killer" myth in 2021, the project erupted, encouraging a sizable number of P2E games and Web3 projects to transition to the Avalanche network.

Although the project's initial buzz has died down in recent months, its technology is still cutting-edge. The incredibly remarkable throughput of Avalanche was one of the key factors in its ability to gain traction so fast.

Avalanche resolves transactions on three distinct chains rather than considering all transactions as one. The greatest

Defi currencies and Web3 applications utilize the C-Chain to settle transactions; X-Chain is used to transfer and receive AVA, and P-Chain is used for network validators. AVAX has significantly declined from its 2021 highs, but the Defi coin bottomed at roughly $20. Following its sharp decline, investor confidence has probably been rattled, but once the next bull run starts, AVAX may provide spectacular gains.

10. Maker: DAO behind the leading stablecoin

Investors may join the decentralized autonomous organization (DAO) that oversees the well-known stablecoin DAI using Maker (MKR), a governance token. MKR could be the greatest Defi cryptocurrency to purchase this year, with the DAI stablecoin fast gaining market share and the algorithmic dollar-pegged stablecoin UST falling out of favor.

The MKR token is meant to provide investors and project supporters value since stablecoins are intended to stay the same (unless something goes wrong). By allowing all MKR holders to vote on DAI's development and linking the price of MKR to DAI's success, this method should ensure that only the best choices are made regarding the stablecoin's future. Maker is the ideal Defi project to invest in since it suits the market so well. The need for a reliable stablecoin is greater than ever; thus, the Defi cryptocurrency may achieve great things shortly.

11. Loopring: advanced layer-2 scaling solution for Ethereum

While there was significant demand for Ethereum substitutes, the attention is now on Layer-2 scaling options like Loopring (LRC). Although these applications use the Ethereum network, they often use other methods to settle transactions. This implies that Layer-2 solutions use Ethereum's security without being constrained by its slow throughput.

Loopring groups many transactions together off-chain before settling them all on-chain to achieve a better throughput than its parent network. Because of this, the project can validate transactions much more quickly than Ethereum, which lowers costs and relieves network congestion.

Loopring has gained notoriety thanks to its collaboration with GameStop. Although it hasn't had a significant shift to the upside, the project has received a lot of attention, making it one of the top Defi ventures to invest in before the market recovers.

12. Uniswap: decentralized exchange and Defi platform

Uniswap (UNI), developed by former Ethereum engineer Hayden Adams, has a long history. Some top Defi projects to invest in are hosted on this decentralized exchange (DEX). The platform gained global prominence during the Defi boom and swiftly rose to become one of the most popular DEXs in the world.

As a governance token, UNI enables supporters of the project to shape its destiny. The fact that Uniswap and PancakeSwap are still among the most popular decentralized trade protocols indicates that this strategy was successful.

With a market valuation of more than $1 billion, Uniswap is no longer regarded as a low-cap cryptocurrency, although DeFi-centric investors continue to appreciate the project. A slump has severely impacted Uniswap's lesser Defi initiatives, but it's probable that if these projects start to receive attention again, Uniswap will see enormous volumes.

13. Compound: well-known platform for borrowing and lending

One of the top Defi crypto ventures to invest in right now is Compound (COMP), a famous lending platform. Holders of the COMP token may vote on policies that impact the plat-form, which is utilized for governance. Compound manages a variety of pools, making it simple for investors to earn interest on their cryptocurrency holdings.

To avoid issues with capital gains, the platform enables users to safely utilize their bitcoin as collateral to get a fiat loan. While the Compound platform assures security, users can also earn interest on their assets by lending them to others.

It's certainly feasible that COMP might be one of the finest Defi cryptos to watch this year, given that Compound is one of the most well-liked platforms for lending and borrowing cryp-tocurrency assets and that the industry is quickly growing popularity.

14. Terra Classic: legacy pumping project Defi

Following the debut of the brand-new LUNA token, Terra Classic (LUNC), which was born from the demise of the Terra Luna, was produced. The project was once intended to be a platform for lending and yield farming, similar to Compound. However, the demise of Terra's UST stablecoin rendered the original token all but useless.

The LUNC coin was created due to difficult circumstances and additional choices, but its acceptance has since skyrock-eted. Unexpectedly, LUNC has been doing fairly well since its debut. The token, one of the best-performing investments in recent months, has grown by an astounding 376% since its launch in June and an equally astounding 183% over the previous month. Although the project's value as a safe place to keep tokens and receive a payout has been severely diminished, it still holds as one of the top Defi investments currently available.

Advice for newcomers before buying Defi coins

As this is your first venture into the world of cryptocurrencies, it is recommended that you begin balancing your portfolio immediately. Remember to invest a portion of your income in cryptocurrencies, particularly an amount you can afford to lose. If you do so, don't worry too much. These are broad suggestions to improve your long-term results and prevent being taken advantage of, not financial advice.

Bottom line

For several reasons, purchasing decentralized finance coins can be wise. Always investigate how to invest in DeFi thoroughly and review as many DeFi exchanges as possible. DeFi financing and DeFi farming are also options, but you must take those risks.

You choose to invest in the token's value increasing over time and the numerous use cases provided by the projects in exchange for access to governance rights within the project.

The long-term value of this investing technique is very high. However, remember that this is not financial advice, so it is up to you to determine your aspirations and individual investing goals. Join Zipmex today to take the first step.

Top 5 Defi Stocks to Keep an Eye on in 2023

One can only assume that the popularity of Defi will increase with bitcoin even as the world pays greater attention to blockchain solutions. The following is a list of what we believe to be the finest Defi stocks to watch in 2023. According to the state of the market, each will be evaluated for its potential for both short- and long-term investment.

Riot Blockchain, Inc. (RIOT)

Cryptocurrency mining is another sector within the cryptocurrency market that is anticipated to gain prominence and significance over time. Large-scale mining facilities support Bitcoin mining by Riot Blockchain, Inc. throughout the US. Let's examine its potential for trading and investment:

- Even while RIOT has a thrilling sensation for investors, it is a high-risk company with a lot of volatility and is not the best choice for long-term investment.
- RIOT's price is highly correlated with Bitcoin's, providing traders with more information about trends and enabling them to plan their positions for short-term trading better.

Investors have an alternate method to participate in the flourishing cryptocurrency evolution with blockchain stocks like RIOT (as opposed to buying or trading cryptocurrency or crypto CFDs).

Canaan, Inc. (CAN)

Canaan Inc., a crypto-mining play similar to RIOT, may intrigue traders and investors seeking to diversify in the Defi stock arena. This publicly traded company focuses on the high-computing technologies required to address the complex problems associated with cryptocurrency mining.

- A day trader or swing trader with knowledge of the blockchain sector may find the company's 52-week range of $3.50 to $39,10. This assumes the trader can keep up with the stock price and is comfortable with the company's level of risk.

- The company is based in China. Long-term investment potential is extremely risky given China's stance on cryptocurrencies. (However, the company could technically diversify outside of this sector.)

Canaan, Inc. may succeed, as with many businesses in this developing and competitive economic sector (or a miss). What do you think of CAN as the best Defi stock? Utilize our Invest.MT5 platform right now to invest in Canaan, Inc.

CoinBase Global, Inc. (COIN)

In the Defi community, CoinBase has continued to be one of the most well-liked and in-demand publicly traded firms, just as it continues to be one of the most well-liked cryptocurrency exchanges.

- Given that Q4 2021 earnings are anticipated to be $2.16 per share on $1.98 billion in revenue (as reported on 24 February 22), it might be advantageous to keep a comfortable amount of COIN for the long run.
- Well-positioned short-term bets may be a viable trading strategy in the ensuing months of 2023, given COIN's volatility and its related industry.

ProShares Bitcoin strategy ETF CFD (BITO)

For the cryptocurrency community, the debut of the first Bitcoin ETF in 2021 was huge news. This incident signaled a new step in accepting cryptocurrencies as investment vehicles.

- With a current share price of roughly $25 and a 52-week range of $20.90 to 44.29 as of February 2023, this could be a suitable entry point for both short- and long-term trades with BITO.
- Given the current unpredictability and future regulation of cryptocurrencies, this might be detrimental to the performance of the ETF or a haven if you want a secure vehicle in the crypto market.

Users with accounts at Admiral Markets AS Jordan, Ltd and Admiral Markets Pty, Ltd can access BITO through our Invest.MT5 account.

Polygon (MATIC)

Web 3.0 is a hot topic right now, with all technological developments heading in one direction or another. The ultimate scaling platform for Ethereum's dApps, Polygon, may have saved the best for last, and it is undoubtedly one of the main current forces driving the Defi ecosystem. Consider that:

• Polygon has competition from Polkadot, Chainlink, and Cardano. Therefore this should be considered while formulating a plan including this class of assets.

• MATIC's current price range of $1.20-2 makes it a good candidate for a broad number of tactics and positions in the short and long term.

Will Polygon (MATIC), one of the top 5 Defi stocks to watch in 2023, perform well? At Admirals, you can trade with the MATIC CFD right now.

Are Defi stocks worth it?

Time will always tell which businesses (and currencies) will take the lead for both the short- and long-terms in any new vertical or sub-vertical in the markets. When deciding whether or not to trade or invest in the potentially top Defi stocks for 2023, it is essential to remember that Defi, like many other similar industries, is still in the development stage.

As you have discovered, the potential of Defi extends beyond only investing in the industry's publicly traded companies; other choices, such as ETFs and currencies, will undoubtedly become available as the sector develops.

Key features in this chapter

- It covers how to invest in DeFi, outlines several prospects, and provides a straightforward step-by-step guide.
- It would help if you bought the proper DeFi coins or tokens once you've decided on the DeFi protocol you want to invest in.
- Another option to diversify your DeFi holdings would be to invest in liquidity pools.
- Within days of the pre-sale beginning, the project received an outstanding response, raising more than $2 million in less than a week.
- The next-best Defi token to buy for 2023 is D2T, the native cryptocurrency of the Dash 2 Trade crypto analytics and intelligence platform.
- New coin available in exciting presale: C+Charge is a cutting-edge ecosystem that gives carbon credits to electric vehicle (EV) owners who charge their cars.
- When deciding whether or not to trade or invest in the potentially top Defi stocks for 2023, it is essential to remember that Defi, like many other similar industries, is still in the development stage.

7

DEFI AND WEB3

onations are down 24%. However, the decentralized
sector has survived a challenging year. It is not
surprising that DeFi and Web-3 fundraising have
suffered in a year marred by a bear market and numerous cryptocurrency scandals. But what is really startling is how much
money is still being invested in the expanding industry.

According to investment data source CB Insights, venture
capitalists and other investors invested close to $3 billion in
firms related to DeFi, NFTs, and the Metaverse in the third
quarter. Even if that represents a 24% decrease from the second
quarter, it still exceeds the $2.7B that investors invested in the
decentralized sector at the same time last year.

Improvement

According to CB Insights, funding for blockchain initiatives
is projected to reach a record $29B in 2022, an increase of 10%
from the previous year. But hold off on popping the corks just
yet. In November, the fall of FTX, the world's No. 2 cryptocurrency exchange, shattered trust in the blockchain industry.

According to DeFi Llama data, funding for DeFi is currently only one-seventh the level in November of 2021, the peak of DeFi investing, with $1B raised.

Famous cryptocurrency analyst DeFi Ignas published a graphic demonstrating a strong association between the price of Bitcoin and monthly fundraising totals, starting in the second half of 2020. According to the researcher, fewer than half as many Web3 projects completed 65 financing rounds in November as they did in the same month in 2021.

Per CB Insights, funding for DeFi and Web-3 startups totaled more than $23B during the first quarter of 2021. Moreover, according to data provided by CB Insights and published by Ben Lakoff, producer of the Crypto Mondays podcast, overall VC funding has reached its lowest level since the first half of 2020. Web3 and DeFi funding are favorable in this context

The Metaverse, Web3, and DeFi

Blockchain-based Decentralized Finance is a way to conduct financial transactions. In contrast to a bank, which pays the client interest on deposits that it uses to create loans at a slightly higher rate, a DeFi transaction is mediated by a protocol rather than a middleman who collects additional fees for services. DeFi eliminates the bank and instead processes the transactions through a market, resulting in financial savings, speed improvements, and increased security thanks to a blockchain-based transaction.

Emerging technology is characterized by two things: an abundance of conferences and linguistic ambiguity. Immersive computing professionals insist on AR/VR over the all-encompassing XR. Sincerely, no longer nobody cares. There are also fewer conferences dedicated to AR and VR, and now they are talking about Web-3 and Metaverse.

Current uses of Web3 technology

To establish a decentralized open network devoid of gate-keepers like Apple, Amazon, Meta, and Google, Web-3 is a solution to decentralizing the Internet that uses peer-to-peer protocols. Gavin Wood, a co-founder of Ethereum, coined the phrase in 2014, and it gained popularity in 2017 as major technological venture capital firms formed multibillion-dollar funds for new Web3 initiatives.

Otoy, a business that operates covertly in the background of the games and entertainment industries and one you probably have yet to hear of is a good illustration of the decentralizing potential of Web3 technologies. Otoy assists in converting the code-based creations of artists into 60 frames per second, high-resolution 2D or 3D images.

It is known as "rendering". Otoy uses its own "secret sauce" of AI and machine learning to speed up the process and save costs while removing "noise" or errors that might occasionally taint the output. Otoy rents your computing power at night when you're not using your computer. Render tokens (RNDR), which can be exchanged for cash on a cryptocurrency exchange and have a volatile value based on market demand, are used by producers to pay for processing.

Wi-Fi network Helium offers free public Wi-Fi hotspots to users who get rewarded for sharing their connection is another noteworthy Web3 application. These hotspots have a 200 times greater range than most Wi-Fi hotspots. Owners amass the cryptocurrency $HNT, which they can swap for money. A well-known user of the Helium wireless network is Lime Scooters.

The potential of Web3 to disrupt

Shortly, one of the most important and obvious uses of NFTs or tokens may be in the arts and entertainment sector, where

Web3 is currently being deployed. The token grants people access to artwork, film, music, and financial investment. By regulations that eliminate them, studios, labels, and distributors like Spotify and Netflix would be supplanted. A virtual land sale just collected $320 million for the construction of the yet-to-be-created virtual world, Otherside, by the Bored Ape Yacht Club.

Finally, the owner may need to pay the artist when selling the piece based on the smart contract encoded in the blockchain record of the transaction. Artists will now profit if the value increases. Studios and labels may avoid Google and Amazon. Andreessen Horowitz just launched a new $4.5 billion Web3 Fund. The fourth is it. Despite the market collapse in the spring of 2022, they are increasing their crypto investments.

Web3 and an open Metaverse

The spatial 3D Internet, now known as Metaverse, had little to do with Web-3 for over a decade. Somnium Space has its virtual world and cryptocurrency. CUBE, and Decentraland, whose currency is MANA, Web-3, and VR just came together. Axie Infinity is one of the play-to-earn cryptocurrency games available. Sandbox is an open-world game where players can purchase "land" and digital products. Through our 2D interface, similar to a conventional video game like the Fortnite game metaverse, we move about in various 3D worlds.

Boson Protocol has developed a mechanism for Somnimum Space retail sales that they intend to roll out to various metaverse shops. Manufacturers of luxury goods were among the first to look for Web-3 solutions, and their intermediaries control the consumer relationship and receive a big share of their expensive goods.

Many people support the creation of an open metaverse with protocols for e-commerce, user-generated content, and an open market for the cross-platform exchange of digital products and services. For businesses like Meta, these kinds of disintermediating technologies are bad news. With user data, it will be much easier to monetize people. Consumers, on the other hand, gain a lot from centralization. Apple and Google charge for services others can offer more readily and even more effectively but at a lower cost.

A different meaning of Web3

In their famous book The Fourth Transformation from 2016, Shel Israel and Robert Scoble outline the four stages of computing development: (1) PC (2) internet (3) mobile, and (4) new, emergent spatial computing. This is different from Web-3, which distinguishes between the three phases of the Internet and computing. Although difficult to use and relied on protocols, Web-1 (or was it Web 1.0?) was open and decentralized. Big tech firms like Amazon and Google, who make enormous sums of money from our data and the user-generated material we voluntarily provide, govern Web-2 (the present Internet). Web-3 wants to alter all of that.

In our talk over lunch, a Microsoft executive repeated the term "Web-3" so frequently that I had to ask him what he meant. To be completely honest," he replied. "I'm not certain. Everyone I speak with substitutes "Web-3" for "metaverse." Meta currently owns the Metaverse, and they chose the name for that reason. Very true. You must include Meta after the word "metaverse" each time.

Ironically, just before the announcement of the Facebook name change, Zuckerberg said his company was approaching its work in the Metaverse with "humility and openness." Still, he didn't realize he was doing the opposite by seizing the word Meta minutes later.

Janko Roettgers questioned Zuckerberg in a May 2022 interview with Protocol about Meta's branding, "which demonstrates an intent to control the Metaverse. According to Zuckerberg, "By taking these actions and selecting that name, we made it quite obvious what we intended the firm to be focused on. Zuckerberg continued by pointing out that Fortnite and Nvidia are developing their versions of the Metaverse, proving it is not a monopoly.

The second meaning of Web3 has developed from my contact with Microsoft's visceral response to the Meta Metaverse. Writing "Meta Metaverse" has the feeling of capitulation, and Web3 is easily pronounced. For these reasons, "Web-3" may someday replace "Metaverse."

Unlimited possibilities, unheard of risk

There is a purpose for centralization. Apple, Google, Meta, Amazon, and Microsoft have all made enormous investments in platform centralization. I give Google and Apple $2.99 per month each, and I wouldn't mind paying more. Additionally, incumbents won't do anything but watch. They are working on projects with this technology and have the resources to do so.

However, it is also simple to see how the financial markets might be affected. Trillions of dollars, if not entire economies, are on the line. This kind of market disruption could result in the birth of the next Google. These possibilities are producing strong incentives for innovation. Web3 is focused on games or some aspect of e-commerce, but it is much more than that.

There is a lot of activity on the so-called Web3. Given that blockchain was in the tank and rising out of an abyss a few years ago, it's brilliant marketing. Tony Parisi, a former executive at Unity who is now a Web3 consultant, said, "Yes, there is the customary marketing hype, but it exists because blockchain is being used for these enormous, revolutionary reasons.

Outstanding technology is now being developed. The poor user experience is preventing widespread adoption. Include all the theft and fraud as well. Parsing it all out is difficult."

Anonymity is innate to the cryptographic system. Because it absolves people of accountability, there are better options for a marketplace. The developers of Bored Apes tokens will be fine if it takes them a long time to make a cheap, unattractive planet you wouldn't want to dwell in if the land were free. Following a $650M cryptocurrency theft, the Vietnam-based Web3 game Axie Infinity had to issue additional digital money to prevent the collapse of its tokens.

Venture investors also received a portion of their profits, allowing them to start making money much sooner than they would have been allowed in a controlled market. Cryptocurrency is one of the most unpredictable and hazardous investments an investor can make. However, that will only sometimes be the case due to perverse incentives and a need for more transparency. It also utilizes Web3 technologies.

Key features in this chapter

- According to investment data source CB Insights, venture capitalists and other investors invested close to $3 billion in firms related to DeFi, NFTs, and the Metaverse in the third quarter.
- Improvement according to CB Insights, funding for blockchain initiatives is projected to reach a record $29B in 2022, an increase of 10% from the previous year.
- According to CB Insights, funding for DeFi and Web3 startups totaled more than $23B during the first quarter of 2021.
- The Metaverse, Web3, and DeFi Blockchain-based Decentralized Finance is a way to conduct financial transactions.

8

THE RADFI KEYNOTE EVENT: THE RADIX ENGINE CAN CHANGE DEFINE DEFINITION FOREVER

P iers Ridyard, the CEO of Radix, introduced their most recent innovations, the Radix Engine and Scrypto programming language, designed specifically for quick and simple Web-3 development.

These two technologies, according to Radix, have the potential to alter the entire DeFi sector fundamentally. Ridyard outlined the space's shortcomings, pointing out that it was difficult to navigate and lacked UX components, which he used to illustrate the present problems in the DeFi sector. Developers, regular users, and entrepreneurs need to embrace the field with usability because they believe it is too complex to scale successfully.

The speech addressed how developers played a crucial part in launching a technological ecosystem and described their strategy for boosting DeFi adoption by changing the environment for developers working in the field.

Let's now analyze their event and show how the Radix Engine is poised to become the standard for DeFi.

The state of decentralized finance right now

With a valuation of close to 12 billion USD, the current CAGR rate of 42.1% for the US market is even more impressive. Nevertheless, despite the anticipated increase, DeFi needs more regional developers.

Around 20,000 smart contract developers actively work in the DeFi space; that's a strong beginning. However, as compared to the 27.7 million developers that labor globally, this number hardly makes a dent. The same is true of how the general public views DeFi. Even while those of us who are actively involved in this community are constantly exposed to news about blockchain, only a few people are aware of what DeFi is.

How many people you know understand DeFi? Do you know anyone who utilizes DeFi as their primary banking system in addition to owning cryptocurrencies? DeFi poor usability is the leading cause of its low utilization. This technology will only ever be able to match CeFi in terms of usability with an intuitive interface.

The lack of resources is a significant factor in the need for DeFi adoption from a developer perspective. The development and widespread use of Unity and Unreal leveled the playing field in the gaming business. New developers could handle bugs independently because they had immediate access to various reusable visual and digital elements that sped up production.

Due to this accessibility, programmers from all over the world began to swarm to this area. This sparked a surge of interest among entrepreneurs and led to an era of spectacular expansion for the gaming industry. Gaming became a global leader quickly, surpassing other industry juggernauts like TV and music.

Gaming is currently worth over 220 billion USD and is expanding at a 12.9% CAGR daily. The accessibility, and organization greatly fuel this remarkable growth and support technologies like Unreal and Unity provide.

In light of this, Ridyard disclosed that Radix does not think a lack of technology is to blame for the lack of adoption within DeFi development. Developers are staying away instead due to the difficulties and lack of accessible support mechanisms. Developers would be equipped with all the resources required to prosper in this ecosystem if DeFi offered anything akin to Unity or Unreal.

How Radix will transform the DeFi sector

The issues raised above are what Radix explained in their speech about why Web-3 has yet to take off. After that, they disclosed that they had been resolving these issues head-on within DeFi since December 2021.

The Radix Engine, an all-in-one system that eliminates the low-level, tedious effort associated with creating Web-3 ecosystems, was discussed by Radix. Radix merely removes the work that developers will agonize over for 80% of their time. Since asset behavior is woven into the fabric of the engine, dApps and wallets can virtually instantly adapt to new token types.

Wallets, applications, and tokens may instantly connect rather than battling for interoperable connections. The first Web 3-build development engine enters the globe with this announcement from Radix. In front of our eyes, Radix is transforming DeFi into the game industry that Unity and Unreal did. This insight was not isolated; Radix immediately began using a new programming language created expressly for their engine.

Scrypto – A Web 3.0 programming language

The platform sought to maximize the developer experience to realize the Radix engine's promise fully. They required a programming language created for and integrated into the fabric of the engine itself to provide the finest solution possible.

Similar to how JavaScript made it possible for Web developers to communicate with browsers without constantly switching between the server and the page, Radix suggests a new language to make it easier to build inside the Radix Engine.

Scrypto, their programming language, was developed with Web 3.0 in mind. An intuitive coding system is provided through seamless integration into the Radix Engine, enabling developers to build and deploy in only a few seconds. The user experience had to come first if this was to succeed, as Radix highlighted in their keynote.

Scrypto will be the driving force behind Web-3, just as Javascript transformed Web-1 into Web-2, giving access to businesses like Facebook, Twitter, and YouTube to rule that market. After more than a year of preparation and improvement, Radix has already tested its Radix engine with more than 4,500 developers.

Most early development participants have been enthusiastic, praising the language and engine as innovative. As a Google software engineer said, "I would rank this among the top languages for computer programming."

The Radix Engine and Scrypto outperform other languages and ecosystems in the Web-3 realm, enabling developers to design the DeFi world they desire quickly.

The Future is bright for Web-3

The Radix one was one of the most important keynotes we've ever seen at a DeFi event. Radix has gone further than anyone before them by proposing and implementing a new DeFi engine that employs its programming language. The blockchain developer community flocked to the engine to test it out, and the event has already attracted media attention. The Radix Engine has all the makings of game-changing technology, despite still being in its infancy.

Key features of this chapter

- Piers Ridyard, the CEO of Radix, introduced their most recent innovations, the Radix Engine and Scrypto programming language, designed specifically for quick and simple Web-3 development.
- The Radix Engine, an all-in-one system that eliminates the low-level, tedious effort associated with creating Web 3 ecosystems, was discussed by Radix.
- After more than a year of preparation and improvement, Radix has already tested its Radix engine with more than 4,500 developers.
- The group aimed to create a decentralized economy with various DeFi goods and services.

9

DEFI PREDICTIONS: HOW WILL BLOCKCHAIN AND CRYPTOCURRENCY CHANGE IN 2023?

Without question, 2022 was a fairly down year for the DeFi and crypto industries. Scams, and hacking have severely damaged the trust in the sector with rug pulls and other illegal activities. The market sentiment for cryptocurrencies was notably negative compared to the preceding two years. Additionally, this slowed the development of the blockchain and DeFi protocols.

It's critical to examine some key industry projections for 2023 to understand how the market may change or develop in the upcoming year.

The positives gleaned from 2022

The year 2022 wasn't been entirely depressing and terrible. The use of blockchain has increased across all industries. In particular, the banking sector expanded its blockchain market share from 11% to 29.7% during that year. JPMorgan's largest banking and financial services company completed its first blockchain transaction on the Polygon network last month. This year, Citigroup also upped its blockchain investment.

Additionally, the year saw an increase in the adjusted TVL (total value locked) for DeFi protocols from $60 billion to $142 billion. Ethereum was the primary blockchain network for all active and upcoming DeFi initiatives in 2021. Despite Ethereum's continued dominance in 2022, other rival blockchains like Solana and Polygon saw a surge in market share.

Top cryptocurrency and DeFi predictions for 2023
Regulation is inevitable

This year, scams and hacks have rocked the current business, from Celcius to the FTX exchange. Users have lost more than $1 billion due to the most recent FTX crash alone. Major cryptocurrency investment platforms like BlockFi have also declared bankruptcy since there aren't enough funds to support user withdrawals.

The popularity of these events in 2023 has unavoidably prompted worries about additional rules for the sector. The CEO of Binance, CZ, has previously released a statement in favor of the requirement for increased regulatory oversight of centralized exchanges.

Along with other G20 nations, US President Joe Biden has advocated for a comprehensive regulatory framework for digital assets and transactions. According to these developments and the industry's current condition, the number of rules governing crypto and DeFi advertising will likely expand substantially in 2023.

DEXs (decentralized exchanges) will become more popular.

The year's ongoing demise of centralized exchanges has demonstrated the importance of transparency and control in this sector. Many users have discovered that it is unwise to put their money in the hands of centralized exchanges.

Even though DEXs are frequently complicated and call for more research from the typical user, these platforms provide total transparency and control. Users have complete visibility over how their assets are stored or invested within the platform. Thus, they are not required to hand over their money to a business. As a result, 2023 and onward could be a turning point for DEXs. We may also see the introduction of new features in DEX platforms and applications.

Stablecoins will be under scrutiny

The market has grown very wary of stablecoins that don't have enough audit processes to confirm their assets and preserve their dollar peg after the colossal disaster of Terra LUNA and its UST stablecoin. In 2022, several tier-2 stablecoins failed due to a lack of user interaction and adoption. Given the minimal likelihood of additional stablecoins entering the market in 2023, such monitoring may continue. The market may continue to be dominated by Tether and USDC.

Ethereum to perform better than Bitcoin?

ETH is expected to exceed BTC in growth and scalability in 2023. The long-awaited Ethereum merge finally occurred in September this year, switching the network's consensus process from the power-hungry mining-based Proof-of-Work (PoW) architecture to Proof-of-Stake (PoS). This has increased the sustainability of the well-known blockchain and drastically decreased the supply of ETH tokens. This should benefit ETH in 2023, and the network's greater adaptability may enable Ethereum to surpass Bitcoin in performance.

In general, 2023 is anticipated to be a significant year for blockchain, cryptocurrencies, and DeFi. The community will hope for an improvement going into the new year as the market mood continues to be weak.

Top 5 DeFi Trends for the Years 2023–2024

Now you will learn about the most significant trends in the DeFi industry.

1. Traditional financial instruments enter the DeFi landscape: Some estimate that the overall value of financial derivatives in the traditional financial markets is ten times more than the global GDP. In essence, the value of derivatives dwarfs that of conventional financial markets. Conversely, the DeFi derivatives market is still developing.

The market for DeFi derivatives now has a $27.81 billion TVL, but its recent development has been striking. By the end of 2020, the TVL of the DeFi derivatives market was about $25 billion.

The dominant company in this market is Maker. Over 27% of the market for DeFi derivatives is made up of it. At the moment, Uniswap is ranked second on the DeFi derivatives market table.

Wrapped Bitcoin (WBTC) is another example of how the cryptocurrency business has used derivatives to boost productivity. WBTC is a method for producing a bitcoin derivative based on Ethereum.

The derivative form of the bitcoins that Bitcoin users hold can then be used to lend, stake, or yield farm on the Ethereum blockchain. The supply of WBTC increased from 600 BTC to 124,000 BTC in 2020. Even packaged Ethereum is available (WETH).

Following the introduction of ETH, the ERC-20 token standard (now utilized in most smart contract transactions) was developed. As a result, many ETH owners desire to turn their currency into an ERC-20 token. WETH makes this possible for ETH owners. And it is well-liked. Over 5% of ETH was said to have been converted into WETH as of September 2020. And more than 5.5 million WETH had been produced by the end of 2020.

From the world of traditional finance to the crypto environment, tranche lending is one type of financial innovation. Tranche lending products, which are used in the financial industry, enable lenders to finance more variable and riskier loans by taking a pool of loans and distributing the revenues to different groups of investors based on risk tolerance. The exposure to assets is spread out. Additionally, risk exposure is a choice made by the owners of the tranche lending instrument.

While investors desiring a larger return are compensated with riskier income that may or may not be paid, lower-risk investors are paid with the aggregate interest first. Tranche lending is being invented in cryptocurrency by protocols like BarnBridge and Saffron Finance.

The cryptocurrency community is more dependent upon this than ever. With the development of several tranche lending methods, it is easier to obtain consistent guaranteed income because of the inherent volatility of crypto assets.

The development of DeFi insurance is directly tied to the expansion of DeFi and its derivative products. These insurance agreements share several characteristics with conventional insurance. However, DeFi insurance works completely decentralized by pairing DeFi users who want to earn money with those who want to lower risk.

For instance, Nexus Mutual is a DeFi insurance platform that enables ETH owners to pool their money to offer insurance for additional smart contracts. If the danger insured by the insurance materializes, the insurance buyers will receive a payout after contributing to this pool.

By February 2021, Nexus Mutual had increased from about $4 million TVL in July 2020 to about $250 million TVL. and doubled every year until reaching more than $500 million in February 2022. Additionally, Bridge Mutual provides a simple approach for anyone to protect their assets by obtaining coverage or to generate interest by offering coverage.

Bridge Mutual offers peer-to-peer insurance protection for stablecoins, cryptocurrency exchanges, and smart contracts, similar to Nexus Mutual. The platform raised $1.6 million in a private offering that received a $9 million oversubscription. Financial products, including insurance, derivatives, and tranche or collateralized lending, should become more significant as the DeFi market expands.

2. DeFi Seeks to monetize blockchain gaming

Globally, there are more than 3 billion players. They spend more than $159 billion annually, projected to reach about $256 billion by 2025. Players and creators seek to monetize the business better as more and more people invest hours in this entertainment.

Blockchain gaming is one strategy developers are attempting to use to make money. These video games run on a blockchain rather than a centralized server. Additionally, players can "mine" tokens by completing specific game tasks.

In-game transferability will require well-known DeFi protocols. Additionally, many gamers' cryptocurrency owners will presumably want a return on their investment. According to a Toptal survey, 82% of developers and 62% of gamers expressed interest in generating and purchasing digital goods that may be traded between games. Since then, the cryptosphere has evolved to meet their needs. Ubisoft developed the first blockchain video game, HashCraft, in 2019. And currently, numerous titles have been published.

BitSport, a platform for cryptocurrency gaming, announced in 2020 that cryptocurrency owners would soon be able to support professional athletes and participate in tournaments. BitSport stablecoin owners can stake their tokens on fresh competitions to generate interest. Or they might support a gambler and receive a cut of their gains.

3. Cross-chain technology aims to address issues with scalability

The rising transaction costs in the DeFi ecosystem are one of the issues brought on by its rapid expansion. The fast-rising Ethereum gas fees are just one illustration of this. In essence, Ethereum gas is the fee needed to complete a transaction on the Ethereum blockchain.

The cost is determined by the supply and demand for the computing resources required to handle network transactions. Since the end of 2020, the average transaction charge has rapidly increased and even exceeded $69 in May of 2021.

The high gas prices may have contributed to the record-breaking DeFi liquidations on February 22 and 23, 2021. The influx of new users using DeFi applications on the Ethereum blockchain has increased transaction costs and slowed the entire network.

Numerous cryptocurrency projects are beginning to offer the cross-chain capability to solve this problem. Cross-chain technology aims to make it possible for transactions and smart contracts to move between chains.

DeFi platforms are expected to scale considerably more readily than they do on the Ethereum network because of this compatibility. Polkadot has been the most successful innovator in this field. In essence, the Polkadot network enables the transfer of currencies, data, and other assets across blockchains. Additionally, it allows users to design unique blockchains.

Additionally, dispersing transactions among several rival blockchains increases their efficiency. The Polkadot Governance Coin (DOT) price increased from less than $10 in August 2021 to more than $50 at its 2021 peak. On top of Polkadot's network, a few DeFi applications have already been developed. The most well-known is undoubtedly Equilibrium.

In 2020, it switched over to the Polkadot network. Equilibrium pledges to develop an open DeFi environment where users can trade assets, lend money, stake assets, and develop smart contracts on several blockchains. And in February 2021, Equilibrium made progress toward this objective. It declared that the largest automated market maker (AMM) for cryptocurrencies, Curve Finance, would establish an exchange on the Polkadot network.

In February 2021, Avalanche, a different network of many blockchains, debuted its Avalanche-Ethereum Bridge platform. The platform provides a new DeFi network with cheaper and more effective transactions. The initiative wants to draw its decentralized applications (Dapps), such as the decentralized exchange Pangolin.

Interoperability between chains has been a successful move for the Poly Network. It has partnered with Binance, the biggest cryptocurrency exchange in the world, to enable the use of Dapps created on either the Poly Network or the Binance Smart Chain across both platforms. The Blockchain Services Network (BSC) has also utilized the Poly Network to accomplish cross-chain interoperability. The Chinese government operates the BSC, which is being utilized to develop an "internet of blockchains."

4. DEX's and AMM's fuel growth in DeFi

Finding a balance between decentralization and efficiency is one of the more challenging issues facing the decentralized finance sector. The use of centralized bitcoin exchanges like Coinbase makes transactions efficient. However, since Coinbase is now a publicly traded firm, they need more decentralization.

Decentralized exchanges (DEXs) are helpful in this situation. Crypto owners conduct direct transactions with one another on DEXs, and there is no requirement to use an intermediary.

As discussed on cryptocurrency trends, Uniswap is the biggest DEX in this market. Uniswap and Curve, the second-largest exchange, account for around 61.6% of all DEX trading volume on DEXs. Additionally, practically all DEX platforms are expanding significantly. The overall amount of DEX trading in January 2021 exceeded $60 billion, a record. DEX trading volume increased more in the first two months of 2021 than in all previous combined. DEXs had to figure out how to improve the efficiency of their decentralized exchanges as volume increased.

They have primarily achieved this by utilizing automated market makers (AMMs). AMMs are primarily employed to offer liquidity on DEXs. On a conventional exchange, bids and ask prices are submitted by buyers and sellers via an order book, and the trade is cleared by the exchange at the best possible price. AMMs offer liquidity pools on a DEX. This incorporates staking, just like the majority of the DeFi ecosystem.

In exchange for interest, owners of cryptocurrencies like ETH lend such assets to the liquidity pool. The AMM collects transaction fees paid by exchange traders to the DEX. Then, interest is paid to the legal owners of the assets in the liquidity pool using those fees. The AMM decides how the pool will be traded based on an algorithm.

According to some experts, this trading strategy has significantly increased DEX liquidity. In reality, 93% of all DEXs now use AMMs, according to Consensys research from November 2020.

The most prosperous DEX, Uniswap, is a good illustration; in fact, it was the very first AMM to be decentralized. And if the growth of Uniswap is any indication, the AMM approach seems effective.

Curve Finance, however, has the highest AMM by TVL (essentially the amount staked in liquidity pools). Curve Finance, which only began operations in January 2020, has seen its total TVL increase from virtually nothing to over $11 billion in a little more than two years.

The stablecoin exchange Curve may be one of the factors attracting crypto-asset owners to the platform. Stakers may anticipate earning a more consistent yield because of the assets' stability.

5. Governance tokens gain in relevance

You may have noticed that the expanding network of DeFi hotspots each has its token. Governmental tokens are of this kind. These tokens differ from conventional cryptocurrencies in several ways. Their main objective is to give token owners voting power over an underlying DeFi protocol.

For example, a DeFi project like Compound could permit users to lend and yield farms using tokens native to a different protocol. However, the Compound also has its token (COMP). And the Compound DeFi protocol is controlled by this token.

Voting occurs on initiatives, and when the DeFi protocol gets more users or raises its TVL, the value of the tokens held by token holders typically increases. And if the pricing is any indication, 2022 has seen a massive increase in interest in governance tokens.

Since the beginning of 2021, the governance tokens for the top three DeFi platforms by TVL have seen a significant price increase. At the start of 2020, MakerDAO has seen its token (MKR) increase by roughly seven times. These tokens are a component of the decentralized autonomous organization's ecosystem (DAOs). The core of DAOs, fully decentralized cryptocurrency networks, are governance tokens.

Take Balancer as an illustration. It is a decentralized exchange for digital assets (DEX). Balancer also developed its governance token, called BAL, which it gives to liquidity providers. Coin owners can trade their tokens with other users and vote on platform proposals. The token's value grows along with the platform as a whole.

Another DEX, Curve Finance, introduced its governance token (CRV) in 2020. Instead of conducting some IPO, Curve issued CRV to the platform's current liquidity providers. The value of owning governance tokens is also beginning to be recognized by conventional financial institutions.

The three companies hold the COMP governance token of Compoundnies with the greatest holdings: Andreeson Horowitz, Polychain Capital, and Bain Capital Ventures.

The top DeFi trends to monitor between 2022 and 2024 end here. Over the past year, this part of the crypto ecosystem has grown incredibly. More so than cryptography itself, in some ways.

Focusing on improved efficiency is one thing that connects several of these developments. The popularity of Ethereum is causing the network to droop. And several technologies (such as DOT) are attempting to close that gap. In either case, it will be fascinating to observe this area

2022 to 2025 DeFi Coin Price Prediction

Decentralized finance projects had almost $200 million invested in them during the first quarter of 2022, demonstrating the amazing expansion of this sector of the cryptocurrency industry. Along with this expansion, several fascinating projects aim to challenge established systems; the most recent to get the media's attention is DeFi Coin.

This section covers our comprehensive DeFi Coin price prediction, explains the project's potential value, and then explains how to invest in DeFi Coin right now, all within a few minutes.

Price prediction for DeFi coin

After some impressive positive momentum over the past few weeks, the price of the DeFi coin token has recently been hovering around the $0.3578 mark. Let's take a closer look at the long-term prospects of the coin to get an idea of how much profit can come from investing in DEFC:

- End of 2022: DeFi Coin should logically face increased demand for services like swapping and staking now that DeFi Swap is operational. This demand should gradually help drive DEFC higher; according to our projection, the price might reach $0.65 by the end of 2022.
- End of 2023: The DeFi sector continues to grow and does not show any signs of slowing down, is set to entice more and more investors away from established financial institutions. If this happens, according to our DEFC price projection, the currency may be worth $0.95 by the end of 2023.
- End of 2025: In the coming years, DeFi Coin and DeFi [illegible] are likely to keep growing within the DeFi market, [illegible]ing many opportunities for investors to earn returns on [illegible]dings. We predict that the price of DeFi Coin may

reach $1.40 by the end of 2025 since the price of DeFi Coin should logically increase along with this expansion.

Understanding the use cases of the tokens you purchase to add to your portfolio is crucial since they serve as the foundation for their long-term possibilities. In light of this, let's examine the utility of DeFi Coin in more detail:

Decentralized token swapping

One of its main applications is the ability to exchange DeFi coins for various tokens. Because consumers cannot buy cryptocurrency using a credit/debit card or a bank transfer, decentralized exchanges operate differently from centralized platforms. As a result, users are forced to possess cryptocurrency and use it to trade for other tokens.

DEFC may be exchanged into more than 50 different cryptocurrencies using the DeFi Swap market. DeFi Swap can connect to several popular cryptocurrency wallets, enabling the exchange procedure to be conducted online. As a result, if you own DEFC, you'll have access to many investment opportunities.

Staking and yield farming

Additionally, DeFi Coin is essential to the staking and yield farming services that DeFi Swap provides. Crypto staking is "locking up" your tokens for a set amount to help Proof-of-Stake (PoS) blockchains confirm transactions. You will be able to make a fixed rate of interest by staking your holdings.

Like staking, yield farming entails depositing your tokens in the platform's liquidity pools, providing the liquidity required to support trades between other users. Again, the fixed interest payments you receive through this method are typically far larger than those provided by ordinary bank accounts.

Generating a passive income stream

Last but not least, DeFi Coin is employed to produce a consistent passive income stream. This is accomplished through the taxation system for the token, which compensates DEFC holders for their sustained support of the initiative. The procedure goes like this:

• The tax rate for DEFC buy and sell orders is 10%.

• The remaining token holders receive a total re-distribution of 50% of the tax amount.

• As a result, if $10,000 is returned to DEFC holders and you possess 1% of the total supply, you will be paid $100.

By using this method, token holders will be able to produce returns on par with (or better than) those provided by the finest dividend equities. Those with a lesser risk tolerance will benefit from the taxation's ability to minimize overall volatility.

What influences DeFi coin's price?

DeFi Coin, one of the top low-cap crypto jewels, frequently responds favorably to numerous outside circumstances. Let's talk about three of the primary factors affecting the DEFC price:

Solid community support

Similar to the top meme currencies, the popularity of DeFi Coin among the community significantly impacts its price. Social media platforms that receive much support for a coin generate more substantial buzz about the project. In turn, the token's price rises as more and more small-scale traders buy it.

With over 6,000 members in the DeFi Swap Telegram group, DeFi Coin is already starting to gain traction in this area. Token owners can discuss the project and its price trend on the official subreddit for the token, which has 5,000 members.

Exciting future upgrades

The development team for DeFi Coin and DeFi Swap has several exciting initiatives to advance the ecosystem, as previously revealed. This is essential in the fiercely competitive cryptocurrency market, where new projects are constantly being introduced to carve out a lucrative niche.

A dedicated mobile app, an NFT marketplace, and improvements to the DeFi Swap exchange are all in the team's plans. However, as the exchange develops, other goals will probably come into focus, expanding the use cases for DEFC.

Speculation potential

Finally, the price of the DeFi Coin is affected by speculators who buy and sell the token. This is understandable, considering the noteworthy returns seen recently. However, big buy/sell orders frequently negatively impact the price of a coin with little market value.

But when people are enthusiastic about a token, it can help the price rise significantly. This was demonstrated in the middle of 2021 when investors tried to purchase Dogecoin, resulting in four digits returns. Holders of DEFC shares will be hoping that a similar situation will occur since it could result in exponential gains.

Conclusion of the DeFi Coin price prediction

In conclusion, this DeFi Coin price prediction has touched on all the essential information you need to know about this fascinating project, including why the coin is so highly prized and instructions on buying DEFC right away. DeFi Coin is one of the fascinating cryptocurrency projects this year due to the rapid expansion of the DeFi industry and the token's excellent use cases.

Key features in this chapter

- Without question, 2022 was a fairly down year for the DeFi and crypto industries.
- In general, 2023 is anticipated to be a significant year for blockchain, cryptocurrencies, and DeFi.
- We predict that the price of DeFi Coin may reach $1.40 by the end of 2025 since the price of DeFi Coin should logically increase along with this expansion.
- Tokenized in-game assets can be owned on a blockchain and used to upgrade combat cards or sell for profit.
- Experts predict that Bitcoin will surge in 2023 due to its dominant market position.

10

IS DECENTRALIZED FINANCE THE WAY OF THE FUTURE?

T his alternative global financial system, based on open blockchains like Bitcoin and Ethereum, has grown significantly in size and diversity since its beginnings, despite only being established for a few years. Could DeFi change the established financial system as we know it? Let us dissect it.

Not just a crypto buzzword

The centralized banking and finance industry is being challenged by the innovative new financial technology known as DeFi. With DeFi, you, the investor, are solely liable for your money, unlike traditional finance, where a business, bank, or fund is accountable for your funds. It combines several currently available blockchain-related technologies, including digital assets, wallets, and smart contracts, to build a financial ecosystem ready to replace banks, brokers, exchanges, and everyone who oversees and processes financial services.

This is quite appealing to many: DeFi grants a higher efficiency by eliminating the so-called "middlemen." DeFi provides a means to make money with a lot less investment than would be required. While democratizing access and ownership, it also lends itself to more transparency for financial transactions, which benefits the estimated 1.7 billion unbanked people worldwide.

The best of both worlds

Disruption in the financial sector is here to stay. This is a consequence of the rapid development of technology. In a world where time passes much more quickly than usual, it is essential to be quick on your feet, receptive to new information, and strategic in your thinking. We can use blockchain technology as an example in this situation. Initial reluctance to accept came from the banking industry. Large financial institutions are among those that have begun investing in blockchain and cryptocurrency startups.

For DeFi, it's the same deal. Realizing that DeFi is here to stay, conventional financial institutions can join the bandwagon by adopting and adapting the technology. ING Bank well illustrates the opportunity for cooperation in this area. The Dutch bank has examined the benefits and drawbacks of DeFi and published a paper titled "Lessons Learned from Decentralized Finance." After weighing the advantages and disadvantages, ING Bank concludes that centralized and decentralized financial services can work together to attain the "best of both worlds."

What form would this collaboration take? Financial institutions that are centrally managed should, among other things, be open to new ideas and no longer be risk-averse. To ensure the primary benefits of DeFi are maintained, they must actively engage in the creation of regulations.

Legacy financial institutions can start providing DeFi services to the unbanked and underbanked simultaneously.

Banks can reduce the financing gap for Micro, Small, and Medium-Sized Enterprises (MSMEs) by giving customers more access to the blockchain ecosystem through their current banking services.

We might experience advantages like quicker international transactions, chances to make money work harder, and easier access to lending if the blockchain concepts built on DeFi are integrated into the global financial infrastructure.

A Future-proofing opportunity

The contemporary environment has shaped a new type of consumer, and established financial institutions must adapt. Financial institutions need to put the consumer first and start immediately setting the framework for customized, adaptable, and straightforward solutions. They can draw motivation from financial behemoths like Morgan Stanley and Goldman Sachs, which have already laid the groundwork for this cutting-edge, synergistic finance ecosystem.

The potential for DeFi innovation is high, opening the door to novel and more effective approaches to serving customers. DeFi may be the factor that prevents future decentralization of banking systems.

DeFi's Future Beyond Crypto

How "integrated value exchange" will develop in the future, and how decentralized finance is upending the banking sector. Algorithms and decentralized computer programs will soon control value creation, trade, transfer, and transformation into financial instruments and derivatives. As this technology, known as DeFi, replaces old financial infrastructure and ushers in an era of "integrated value exchange," the financial industry, which has historically played this function, will transform.

. . .

DeFi is modernizing the financial sector

DeFi will revolutionize banking and financial services in a similar way that artificial intelligence and machine learning in FinTech is upending the wealth management industry. For instance, the "Robo-advisor" in wealth management commoditized several fundamental financial adviser functions, including portfolio construction and evaluation.

The same "Robo-advisors" that had initially disrupted them were now enabling these businesses to operate more effectively and deal with customers they would not have previously been able to serve, like those with lower incomes. In the meantime, advisors started concentrating on more beneficial services, like comprehensive financial planning. Disruptive innovations frequently have this as their central topic.

In a similar vein, DeFi will commoditize some of the essential services that banks, financial services providers, and even FinTechs already offer, such as lending, and it will allow them to deliver services more effectively, benefiting the final customer. Businesses looking ahead must know where the risks of disruption are. Financial institutions may place a greater emphasis on the customer/investor experience due to Defi's potential to compete much more profitably with some of their core goods and services. (According to Gartner's forecast in Beyond the Bot, "89% of organizations will compete primarily on customer experience" shortly.)

According to Blockspaces co-founder, Gabe Higgins, "Many organizations still have not properly understood the ramifications of DeFi yet, but a few pioneers are guiding the way. Instead of waiting to be disintermediated, established businesses like Shapeshift and Binance, both digital asset exchanges, have embraced DeFi. Financial services will soon have to face the fact that decentralized protocols that allow users greater transparency and control over their assets are replacing their long-established, entrenched services.

There is hope for banks, FinTechs, and anybody else to stay ahead of the curve and develop financial technologies utilizing these new patterns. DeFi protocols can quickly launch unique, differentiated products and services because most of what occurs in this field are produced using open-source technologies.

The beautiful thing about this industry is that a lot of the technology being developed is at the infrastructure and middleware levels, enabling individuals or groups to build useful apps that address particular use cases quickly. This is the reason the DeFi industry was able to increase and develop. Sometimes, developers can create a brand-new product in a matter of days. However, businesses aren't participating at this level yet, which suggests a possibility shortly.

DeFi is based on a distributed ledger infrastructure, as was already mentioned. Building applications on top of distributed systems has the benefit of allowing open access and disabling particular actors, which improves the effectiveness and lowers the cost of many financial use cases. DeFi applications can operate independently from a centralized controller; they are frequently regulated democratically, giving users input over the protocol's or application's development.

Decentralized protocols and/or tokens based on blockchains could replace any centralized financial service or product. Currently, lending and trade are examples of this. For instance, in the DeFi lending industry, the protocol removes intermediaries from the lender matching, risk management, loan provisioning, and ultimate value transfer processes.

Cryptocurrency tokens and blockchain-based algorithms are beginning to replace the requirement for ETFs (Exchange Traded Funds), mutual funds—baskets of assets and equities—

and even hedge funds in the investment management industry, enabling reduced costs and almost no access restrictions.

Consider the use of decentralized protocols or algorithms as an example. Then, all required is a token derivative representing the individual stocks or assets and a computer algorithm that rebalances and/or trades by a set of rules or criteria. Smart contracts make all of this happen automatically (essentially self-executing programs that run on a blockchain).

Finally, since anyone can utilize DeFi protocols, access is democratized. Only those who meet stringent criteria regarding credit, account balances, etc., are given services by banks. Due to the open-source nature of DeFi protocols, anyone with access can use them by default (a device, internet, and a crypto wallet).

According to Tyler Tarsi, CTO of Recursive Research, the internet has provided the first example. People provide value from anywhere globally with a connection, rather than being in a big metropolis. But until now, we have yet to have a reliable method for transferring value in an internet-native way, which is where DeFi infrastructure comes in.

I'm looking forward to this because it will be far more fair and open than the currently existing walled society. Building a new financial system from the ground up is challenging, getting there will take some time. Nonetheless, it will inevitably happen.

What will the future hold?

"All sources of value will be tokenized," says Tarsi, "allowing value to flow between geographies and industries freely....Because DeFi is solely focused on tokens, people in traditional finance frequently doubt it. But the point is being missed. A token, including real estate, social influence, employment, and community participation, can represent anything."

It is not irrational to believe that practically anything will be able to be priced and traded in the future. As a result, we're coining the term "integrated value exchange" to describe a system in which numerous types of value can be traded digitally via decentralized networks at a reasonably low cost and with little friction. Today, we can monetize and/or transact practically anything by representing it as a token. Liquidity is the key issue preventing us from doing this.

Will there be an open market where tokens can be purchased or sold? The innovation of liquidity pools to establish markets—the cornerstone of DeFi—makes transferring value between assets considerably more convenient.

Decentralized trading is made possible by DeFi, which provides and aggregates liquidity across numerous different cryptocurrencies. Instead of matching a buyer and seller at the moment of the transaction, liquidity pools can be created that can be used quickly. DeFi rewards those who offer upfront liquidity to establish markets between different types of assets. An algorithm will decide how the transaction will happen when you want to access some of this liquidity (i.e., how much one should get and at what price for another). The term "Automated Market Makers" describes these algorithms (AMMs).

This phenomenon is intriguing because these liquidity pools can be connected. Liquidity pools may exist between several assets but not necessarily between every single asset. As an illustration, there might be a market (or pool) between Asset A and Asset B as well as between Asset B and Asset C. What happens if we want to change Asset A into Asset C? In the past, you could have been required to locate a buyer or seller for Asset B, complete the deal, and then locate a buyer/seller for Asset C. Trying to make this process happen digitally may be costly, time-consuming, and a source of friction.

Consider a whole business dedicated to processing payments for this reason, but the total amount of assets they trade is still relatively small. However, you could go from Asset A to Asset C considerably more quickly if all of the liquidity was available, and you could frictionlessly "hop" between assets. DeFi makes this possible and can do it over a far wider range of assets at a degree of efficiency higher than what is now feasible.

We can envision how the exchange of a wide range of assets will be possible with very little friction in the future when trillions will likely be locked in DeFi liquidity and where the spider Web of "liquidity-connected assets" gets larger and wider. This would imply that real estate, works of art, and other tangible assets, formerly illiquid, would now have much more liquidity.

This idea creates a new paradigm for the exchange of value. Within the next ten years, you might use a digital wallet of various assets you own to pay at your favorite retailer. You may need to use fiat money (i.e., USD), bitcoin, digital collectibles (i.e., NFTs), or even issue some short-term debt to pay for the remaining portion of the acquisition (i.e., a DeFi loan).

There may come a moment when you can use tokenized representations of the equity in your house to pay for necessities. Given sufficient liquidity, the options for what you can transact with are unlimited since, as Tyler Tarsi noted, tokens can represent anything.

In the future, you would scan your smartphone over the point-of-sale terminal used by the cashier at the checkout counter to initiate a transaction from your universal wallet, which would house all your assets. The assets you chose to use as payment would all be instantly exchanged and given to the merchant in the type of value that the merchant decides to accept.

While there may be additional issues, like determining the value and gaining access to liquidity for certain assets like real estate, to actualize this goal for all asset classes, they are not obstacles that stand in the way of what we are capable of. Integrated value exchange, also known as seamless cross-asset value transfer, will be the way of the future.

The Future of Finance is Decentralized (DeFi)

There are exciting days ahead: Distributed Ledger Technology (DLT), a decentralized database administered by various participants with no single administrator, will soon power financial and commercial applications. The pace of this shift will pick up in 2023.

Decentralized finance and the technology it employs, distributed ledger technology (DLT), will become as indispensable to our daily lives as the internet has become to us. We take the internet for granted, using it for the convenience, accessibility, and speed it provides without stopping to think about how it functions or why we should.

The COVID-19 pandemic has shown the advantages of the internet. It made it possible for us to interact with services, goods, and people and made a move to a remote, contactless global economy easier. The Internet, or Web 2.0, is now developing toward Web 3.0, or distributed ledger technology.

Impacts of decentralized finance on competition, antitrust policy, and economic growth

Decentralized finance, or the use of blockchain technology in financial services, can improve financial market efficiency, encourage competition, make it easier for small enterprises to acquire money, and stimulate economic development. Despite its potential advantages, the technology also poses significant obstacles to user accessibility, fair competition, and law enforcement. Whether the concerns of investors, consumers, and governing authorities can be satisfactorily addressed —

without regulating the technology into inefficiency and disuse in the process — determines how large the developing Defi sector will become.

In this book, we go through a number of the difficulties and issues concerning Defi as well as the top authorities who have considered and acted on those issues. We also look at embedded regulation's potential to act as a link between regulation and innovation.

An overview of traditional and decentralized financial services

$42.98 billion has been committed to Defi contracts as of July 2022. (Defi Pulse, n.d.). Defi systems received much attention and funding between mid-2020 and October 2022. In November 2021, TVL in Defi contracts hit a peak of $107.5 billion. These digital marketplaces have given birth to dangers and opportunities for real-world applications.

New businesses are developing creative ecosystems, enabling entrepreneurs and small businesses to access finance by linking their physical assets to Defi platforms and utilizing them as collateral. For example, consider Centrifuge, a DeFi-based lending protocol that aims to increase the accessibility of alternative loans for small firms and entrepreneurs by providing investors with access to liquidity pools with consistent payouts (Kraken, n.d.).

Streaming royalties, mortgages, and other conventional assets may be converted into non-fungible tokens (NFTs), which can subsequently be used as collateral for loans at competitive interest rates. According to Centrifuge's revolutionary notion of "unlocking liquidity for real-world assets." Centrifuge tokens are bought by investor users using stable-coins to build a liquidity pool for lending to other people.

Defi's effects on competition and antitrust regulations

Economic theory states that when businesses compete for consumers, it results in cheaper pricing, better products and services, more variety, and more innovation. Dominant companies might exploit their market dominance to prevent prospective rivals from joining the market when there is insufficient competition. Due to this, entrepreneurs and small firms need help to compete pretty and convert their ideas into novel products and services. According to Cetorelli et al. (2007), the top four US commercial banks controlled a gradually growing percentage of all bank assets from 1990 to 2004, indicating a concentration risk in the country's financial systems.

Antitrust laws and regulations govern the concentration of economic power to prevent monopolies and unfair business practices (Cornell Law School, n.d.). Market stability, social welfare, and fair competition are made possible by these rules and regulations. In the sections below, we will go through three competition and antitrust issues regarding Defi:

- Open finance
- Decentralized autonomous organization (DAO) architecture
- Entry barriers to financial markets

Barriers to entry

Defi is not anticipated to enter the financial markets smoothly; at first, conventional financial institutions could have an edge. New rivals or services, like those in any other industry, must overcome several obstacles to take market share. Furthermore, since established financial service providers are unwilling to give up their market share, Jin and Vinella (2022) note that they are likely to respond significantly. Defi also runs into specific entry-level challenges, such as high startup costs.

Defi newcomers also need access to the wealth of historical data established financial firms have. Due to the hassle and expense of transferring information from or sharing it with a conventional banking institution, customers may be hesitant to adopt Defi services. As a result, it is anticipated that customers will only embrace Defi services slowly. It often takes users time to understand, believe in, and adjust to new technology. Technological adoption must be more active regarding financial services and customers' financial security.

Actors in the traditional financial system are strong and, obviously, wealthy. Any new rival will be discouraged by the size and complexity of the established financial system. The Boston Consulting Group (2021) estimates that financial assets make up around $250 trillion, or 60%, of the world's net wealth. The Federal Deposit Insurance Corporation (FDIC) covers 4,787 bank institutions in the United States alone. These banks have 82,184 branch offices and oversee $24.066 billion in financial assets (2022).

The biggest bank in the nation, JPMorgan Chase, has more than 51 million digital clients in the US (Green, 2019); by comparison, the largest Defi network, Bitcoin, has less than 15,000 active nodes worldwide (Jin & Vinella, 2022).

The fact that not all users of the financial system trust or use digital technology presents another barrier to entry for Defi. Among other vulnerable groups, older adults, those with a lower socioeconomic status, people who reside in rural regions, and people with less education may have less access to or knowledge of technological equipment that may be used for Defi.

Furthermore, even if individuals have access to this technology, they may need to be more proficient to utilize it. Some people also need help to go online. Because of this, Defi could worsen the financial inclusion divide.

Furthermore, many individuals prefer personal interaction over automated services. When it comes to finances, an in-person encounter may seem more reliable than one that involves software performing its intended function (Mims, 2021). Compared to human contact, the software may some-times be rigid. Consider a phone conversation as an example.

Many consumers choose to talk directly with a corporate person than navigate a robotic voice menu. People need to be more open to change. Thus, Defi platforms must establish trust before customers would use their services. Defi is disadvantaged against conventional financial services, which often include physical facilities and human connections, because of this entrance hurdle.

Finally, established financial service companies can create their blockchain or Defi apps. In addition, rather than going up against Defi startups, they might purchase them. American big banks have already made significant investments in this field, and JPMorgan Chase funds a staff of 50,000 engineers with $12 billion in annual investments in developing technologies. To compete successfully against established players in the finan-cial industry, new Defi service providers will need to overcome both practical and financial obstacles.

Open finance

The phrase "open finance" refers to a trend toward enhancing user financial data's openness, accessibility, and shareability to promote competition in the financial services industry. Open finance platforms, also known as data-porta-bility systems, let customers exchange their financial informa-tion with other service providers, lowering data-driven entry barriers and fostering competition.

Defi can assist. Open financial systems allow for the creation and provision of new services tailored to clients' demands. According to Awrey and Macey (2022), this can level the information playing field and promote competition between established financial institutions and a new generation of companies. Many of them are trying to meet the demands of customers wanting to pay faster, borrow, invest their savings, convert currency, manage their budget, and so on.

According to Zetzsche, Arner, and Buckley (2020), open finance is justified as a policy goal since it addresses market efficiency, economies of scale, and circumstances where data affects competitive power. Over the last ten years, the information technology (IT) markets in the United States and China have gravitated toward oligopoly or monopoly; open financial systems may combat this by preventing industry concentration.

The pools of consumer and supplier data that digital giants Google, Facebook, Amazon, and Alibaba may be considered their key assets (Ramos & Villar, 2018). With this information, businesses may increase customer reach, set pricing, develop new customized services, and improve advertising. According to Patterson (2017), the concentration of knowledge and data encourages monopolistic conduct and market collusion, which raises prices at customers' cost. Through increasing competition in the financial markets, open finance affords a chance to resist the tendency of data accumulation in just one or a few firms and instead benefit consumers.

When deliberately implemented by a jurisdiction, open finance systems may allow customers to exchange their financial data quickly, easily, and securely across banks, investment management businesses, and insurance organizations (Nicholls, 2019). Open finance can reduce barriers to entry, such as the users' need for historical financial data, and reduce the costs and inconveniences associated with switching from traditional financial services to DEFI services. It should make it more feasible for new DEFI service providers to enter the market.

DAO design

Co-founder of Ethereum, Vitalik Buterin, first proposed the idea of a decentralized autonomous organization (DAO) in 2014, a jointly owned, blockchain-governed organization (DAO) pursuing a common goal. The operation of the company and how money is spent are outlined in smart contracts. DAOs are constructed from a network of interconnected smart contracts that, when specific conditions are met, automatically carry out transactions on a blockchain network to achieve the objectives of their members.

A decentralized autonomous organization's purpose is easily understood, according to Buterin (2014): it is an entity that operates autonomously on the internet but also significantly depends on employing people to carry out certain activities that the automaton itself cannot handle.

DAOs may increase competition by improving prices and efficiency for both DAO members and end users, but they may also pose antitrust issues. DAOs can control trade by setting pricing, segmenting markets, exchanging sensitive information, and more via automated decision-making.

A DAO may also make it possible for rivals to work together to choose which goods to offer and how to price them. Furthermore, if a DAO with a profit-oriented architecture were to dominate a market, particularly extremely tiny, it may start acting monopolistic automatically. These actions are as likely to occur in conventional organizations controlled by people, but they could be more challenging to spot in a digital, autonomous, decentralized, and sometimes anonymous environment. As a result, authorities tasked with safeguarding consumers may need help recognizing antitrust crimes and implementing the law due to DAOs.

DAOs promote competition and improve company efficiency. Additionally, they have a desirable internal governance system that uses computerized voting. DAOs may bring up various antitrust problems that the government may need help to resolve.

Defi's Effects on Economic Growth

Potential Advantages

Defi applications, according to the Organization for Economic Cooperation and Development (OECD), can bring about significant economic efficiencies through the transfer of value without the need for dependable centralized intermediaries, resulting in faster and less expensive transaction automation (2022).

Defi allows for lower transaction costs and more transparency since all transactions are made public. Transactions are initiated by data given by the protocol or by external nodes known as "oracles," hence no human intervention is required. Defi also has a multiplier impact on money. Without conventional banks' solvency and liquidity constraints, lending applications may channel short-term funds and give loans on demand.

As a result, there would be more options for short-term loans and startup financing on the market. This might result in more investments, enterprises, and, eventually, higher GDP. As new players from financial services and other sectors join the market, Defi can create new employment.

Defi technology may lessen the risks of financial instability associated with conventional financial institutions, according to the Financial Stability Board (FSB). This worldwide body studies and provides recommendations about the global financial system (2019). The financial system may become more diverse, and supplier concentration may decline due to the anticipated distribution of financial service providers. The failure of a few institutions is no longer a potentially disastrous event for the economy; it may mitigate the too-big-to-fail issue.

Defi also provides security as there is no single point of entry for attacks. A decentralized environment safeguards against cyber threats while maintaining the accuracy of financial records and service accessibility. Interoperability promised by Defi fosters innovation and fosters a thriving financial environment.

Most of the advantages described above involve effectiveness, economic growth, transparency, and security. We then determine if these advantages may exceed any possible hazards and difficulties.

Risks and challenges

Defi has a variety of drawbacks. First, Defi could encourage financial exclusion since people who stand to gain from cheaper, unconventional financial services, such as small- and medium-sized company owners and managers, might need to comprehend Defi systems better to interact with them effectively or at all.

Second, if crypto-asset volatility is not well understood, an unwary user may put their confidence in a dangerous platform and negatively influence their money. Third, users must place their faith in the developers of the Defi platforms' underlying code and in the smart contracts that carry out transactions, even if Defi proponents claim that the system encourages trust via disintermediation and decentralization.

Only some people would possess the necessary technical knowledge to analyze the smart contract or Defi platform code. Defi adoption will thus need that customers put their faith in software developers rather than the regulated financial institutions that serve as the conventional financial system's middlemen.

Although the activity carried out on a Defi network may very well be covered by legislation (such as securities or antitrust law) and come within the purview of a governing agency, the Defiany government does not presently govern Defi networks (in the US, the Securities and Exchange Commission or the Federal Trade Commission).

Decentralized networks are automated, community-governed, and may operate in numerous jurisdictions simultaneously. Therefore it may be challenging to identify the decision-making individuals who can be held accountable for the network results in any one region. It is challenging to provide oversight, accountability, and even legal notice.

Procedures in the existing legal system are created for centralized decision-making entities with physical locations, such as contemporary financial institutions. Defi networks are global organizations with no clearly defined physical location or jurisdiction, and because of this, law enforcement needs clarification and difficulties (OECD, 2022).

Concerns about consumer protection can also exist. Defi networks with governance systems requiring more than 50% of community votes are immune to manipulation by minorities. Still, if the majority of nodes on a network choose to engage in unethical or unlawful behavior, it might have an impact on all members, including customers.

Since Defi does not rely on a custodial system, the worst-case situation here might be fraud and asset embezzlement. Furthermore, despite the criticism of certain participants, it is feasible for the community to decide on and modify current smart contracts inside Defi initiatives. If so, customers may be subject to modifications to the original contract terms they had signed.

Defi could cause problems with dependability and security. Despite what proponents of Defi have said, it is feasible to corrupt a blockchain. The oracles, or the nodes that feed outside data into the blockchain, are the most exposed elements of the chain. False or misleading information might have serious repercussions if it is presented. For instance, if false pricing information is inserted into the blockchain, it may cause significant buys or sells that would not otherwise occur by the rules of the controlling smart contract.

Some users may suffer significant losses, while others may benefit greatly. Furthermore, even when they entail falsified information or scams, these frauds are irreversible due to the permanent nature of the blockchain.

Holding assets on Defi platforms now is much riskier for investors and financial consumers than doing so in regulated, centralized financial institutions. Consumers have no options if a Defi protocol fails since it would be tough to pin out who is to blame. Participants risk losing money since no dispute resolution procedures or error recovery techniques exist. The fact that defiant programmers may start Defi initiatives without any testing or due diligence being required by legislation in any known country increases this danger.

The potential presence of an "admin key" to the platform's code presents another risk to users of Defi systems. When a Defi protocol behaves erratically, developers sometimes preserve an admin key to access and fix the protocol's code. Users face serious dangers when an admin key is available since it may be used at any moment to access user data or modify a protocol's functionality from the ground up.

The admin key might be used by the creators or developers of the application to confiscate an investor's assets unlawfully. In conclusion, even though Defi is essentially decentralized, human participation in its administration may still be necessary due to admin keys and concentrated ownership of voting tokens.

Finally, better user understanding of financial concerns is only sometimes a result of Defi protocols. Although the platform's source code may be open to inspection, the typical user must gain the specialized financial and technical understanding necessary to comprehend the system's inherent hazards. Users need coding expertise and in-depth financial knowledge to fully comprehend the protocol's hazards (OECD, 2022). Even expert users could need help evaluating Defi technologies' financial risks.

Looking forward

Defi is now fraught with complicated concerns. It is still being determined whether its advantages will eventually exceed the hazards for particular users and the difficulties for established legal and economic institutions. Free market innovation or government regulation — or some mix of the two — will be essential to address such dangers and difficulties adequately.

The deployment of blockchain presents fundamental issues for accountability and law enforcement, such as the difficulty of identifying those responsible for errors in a Defi network's automated outputs and the difficulty of finding the appropriate legislation and jurisdiction.

The possibility of Defi being subject to legislation everywhere or everywhere is so troublesome that it would discourage participants from using decentralized financial protocols. RegTech may provide a way to allow DeFi's financial gains, all while addressing user and financial regulator concerns and the significant problem that the rule of law in financial services presents for all parties, including developers, customers, and governments.

RegTech is the term for using technology (hardware and software) to monitor and comply with regulatory requirements. "Embedded supervision" is one RegTech that may provide a regulatory view into Defi networks. By accessing the market's ledger, embedded supervision "allows compliance in decentralized markets to be automatically monitored, reducing the need for enterprises to gather, verify, and send data manually." Legal factors might be included in the Defi code to achieve regulatory screening goals as part of the permission procedures to join the financial markets. In essence, embedded supervision is an automatic type of compliance.

By supporting "embedded regulation," Zetzsche, Arner, and Buckley move one step beyond the embedded supervision notion. According to this strategy, a Defi system's design would have to consider the main regulatory goals of market behavior, integrity, and stability. Each protocol would include regulatory characteristics in its automated structures, requiring the entry of certain data, quality requirements, and other conventional financial regulatory norms.

Embedded regulation may also answer DeFi's jurisdictional ambiguity if a global agreement can be found. Nations could decide, for instance, that a Defi network is governed by the country where its administrator is situated and that the embedded regulatory system is only required to abide by the laws of that country. The difficulty of achieving this comprehensive agreement under the world's nation-state system of government is discussed by Zetzsche, Arner, and Buckley.

Defi can create more effective financial markets and encourage economic expansion. Given antitrust and other legal issues, Defi systems' adaptability to governance via RegTech's integrated regulations is crucial for the efficient operation of the market. However, excessive regulation may deter business ventures, including Defi initiatives, and impose restrictions on the same features that set Defi apart from other financial procedures.

Defi should continue to be as intermediary-free and innovation-stimulating as feasible to preserve its position as an effective alternative to conventional finance systems. It should be implemented only when embedded regulation offers users of Defi protocols clarity and security. In the end, a balance between the need for a regulatory framework and the flexibility to innovate will need to be found.

Blockchain technology is paving the way for lower prices, better security, and more transparency in the financial system via Defi. Still, the sector currently needs to be more organized and more unregulated. A well-balanced, integrated regulatory framework might foster innovation and make the financial system more secure.

In addition to achieving the goals of consumer protection and financial market competitiveness, it may also enable decentralized finance to reach its full potential in terms of cost-effectiveness and access to capital for entrepreneurs and firms.

Organizing the public debate

For consumers, investors, and the economy to profit from Defi, governments and the business sector must overcome several obstacles. The Defi market is far more established than the public legislative framework to cope with it, with a significant amount of money already locked under Defi contracts ($42.98 billion as of July 2022).

The public discussion, however, is starting to take form as to whether and how Defi should be controlled. To examine and address the issues of Defi, the White House, the Securities and Exchange Commission (SEC), and academics have already released organizational principles and subsequent measures.

A White House Executive Order (EOEO) titled, "Ensuring Responsible Development of Digital Assets", was released on March 9, 2022. In addition to encouraging financial inclusion and stability, avoiding criminal activity, and tackling climate change, the directive aims to set a route for reducing the dangers Defi could represent to consumers, investors, and companies.

The EOEO attempts to retain the United States' strategic financial leadership because the US dollar and American financial institutions dominate the global financial system, providing the country with significant economic and national security advantages.

The rising usage of digital assets and Defi exchanges, according to the EOEO, might lead to a rise in cyber risks for consumers, investors, and organizations, as well as crimes, including fraud and theft, privacy and data breaches, abusive activities, and other crimes. The order mandates coordination among federal agencies responsible for national security, economic, legal, environmental, and technical challenges for them to deliver reports to the White House within 180 to 210 days following the order's date. After reviewing the findings, President Biden's administration will suggest specific changes to law and policy within a year.

The authorities must include suggestions in their studies to address Defi's dangers and possible advantages, as well as any regulatory gaps and unique concerns presented by digital assets. The agencies are now putting the finishing touches on their findings and recommendations. The papers are anticipated to advance high standards of openness, confidentiality, and security for Defi systems that are consistent with American national security and economic interests and may assist the US in retaining its position as a global financial markets leader. Changes in law and policy are anticipated for late 2023.

The EOEO also requests that the Federal Reserve chairman look into the possibility of a central bank digital currency (CBDC) using Defi architecture to improve payment system efficiency and reduce costs. The Federal Reserve is specifically tasked with determining whether a USUS CBDC will improve or impair monetary policy's capacity to successfully serve as a crucial macroeconomic stability instrument for the American economy.

The Federal Reserve has also been mandated to study the potential for foreign CBDCs to replace current national currencies and modify the payment system in ways that threaten the dominance of the US financial system internationally.

Similarly, Commissioner Caroline Crenshaw of the SEC recently released a Statement on Defi Risks, Regulations, and Opportunities (2021). It cautions that the present "buyer beware" strategy used by Defi participants, which discloses that Defi is dangerous without giving investors the information they need to evaluate risk probability, is insufficient as a base for the development of the next generation of financial markets.

Markets are prone to corruption, fraud, knowledge asymmetries, and cartel-like behavior without a uniform set of rules and a working mechanism to enforce them. This may eventually undermine investor involvement and trust.

The US capital market is an excellent illustration of how well-regulated markets often prosper. Despite having fewer than 5% of the global population, the US generates more than half of the world's investment capital (Clayton, 2022). US financial markets are the preferred location for most investors looking to raise funds overseas due to their dependability.

American securities laws provide market certainty as well as imposing costs. However, a strong legal framework that offers considerable protection for market players has not yet been implemented in Defi's new "Wild West."

Several government agencies in the US, including the Department of Justice (DOJ), the Financial Crimes Enforcement Network, the Internal Revenue Service, and the SEC, may have future authority over various facets of Defi. Defi investors currently get different protection and information than is typical in other regulated markets.

The SEC has jurisdiction over various Defi participants, activities, and assets since they include securities and behavior linked to securities, as Crenshaw points out in her statement. However, all Defi players subject to SEC jurisdiction have yet to sign up with us (2021).

While specific Defi initiatives may be fine adhering to SEC rules as they are presently implemented, others may need help. Nevertheless, Defi has to be controlled to lower the risk of deceptive or manipulative behavior. According to Crenshaw (2021), the Defi system should enable efficient capital flow to the best initiatives instead of being constrained by hype or exaggerated promises.

Regulations seek to generate shared incentives aligned to benefit the whole system and offer equal chances for the least powerful members in decentralized networks with dispersed control and diverse interests.

The United States has to embrace the benefits offered by Defi, such as quick payments and custody of assets in digital form, as former SEC chairman Jay Clayton said in a column earlier this year (2022). The guidelines for stablecoins as a form of payment and not a security or commodity should be developed by the working group established by the EOEO on "Ensuring Responsible Development of Digital Assets."

To send a strong message, the DOJ should go after lawbreakers while the SEC issues guidelines for the safe keeping of tokenized assets. The worst-case scenario is that the United States does nothing, which would harm both our global financial system and the American economy.

Meet Smart DeFi From FEG Token

Anyone, even you, can create a new economy for a new world with the help of the Smart DeFi token template from FEG.

Smart DeFi token launchpad

The FEG Token team's Smart DeFi is a cutting-edge token launchpad deployer. Early in 2022, Smart DeFi was introduced with assured asset backing.

Decentralized Finance 3.0 users now have access to Smart DeFi, a full token launchpad that offers a fresh perspective on owning tokens that are secure, insured, and interoperable. Many of the security concerns, expenses, and drawbacks of conventionally issuing a new token are addressed with Smart DeFi.

Currently being built and ready for its upgraded version is Smart DeFi 2.0. Early in December, the FEG team published a roadmap that anticipated a release in Q1 2023.

Getting started

The Smart DeFi launchpad is open to anyone who wants to build their multifaceted cryptocurrency. The FEG-made template makes it simple for producers and investors to get started. A token must initially be fully backed by its base asset, which may be provided by its creators or through a presale.

Creators may assure their customers that their money can only be stolen with coding knowledge. To go beyond these launch barriers, creators and investors only require the assistance of programmers or outside organizations. Tokens must be backed by the native token of that change, either ETH or BNB, and can be created on Ethereum (ERC-20) or BNB Chain (BEP-20).

Characteristics of the smart DeFi token

The percentage allocation of growth funds, the length of the liquidity locking period, and the featured asset backing percentage are token attributes that token producers can select. The method is simple and diverse because there are so many configurable possibilities.

The cutting-edge asset backing system is the main characteristic of smart DeFi tokens. Each token produced with the FEG token smart DeFi technology has a separate locked pool of money backing it up completely, and that pool keeps expanding with every transaction so that users may swap the token, giving it an inherent worth.

To access asset backing technology, creators must burn tokens. The item backing pool has an ever-increasing value behind any particular asset because it can never diminish.

Each cryptocurrency has an exchange and is equipped with advanced technology to thwart and stop rug pulls and honeypot frauds. SmartLending, another component of Smart DeFi, enables investors to utilize their holdings as collateral for quick, interest-free loans.

Key smart token characteristics

- Non-reflective or reflective (RFI) options
- Auto-deployed expedites the procedure in a matter of minutes.
- Option for internal presale
- Growth fund % allocation
- Liquidity locking with no minimum requirement
- Bot-blocking measures
- Access to SmartLending without interest that can be used as collateral

- Compatibility with centralized or decentralized exchange
- Modular tokenomics
- Compatible Liquidity Pairing (LP)
- Easy widget for website positioning

Smart DeFi ecosystem

Smart DeFi promotes a more secure and guarded DeFi ecosystem. Creators may reassure their audiences and customers that each token has intrinsic value and is built thanks to the Asset Backing system forever.

The ecosystem for Smart DeFi is focused on efficacy and cost-savings. The cutting-edge technology developed by the FEG team can be used by project managers, enterprises, and other organizations to increase investor trust.

Because each token functions as an exchange within itself, the Smart DeFi technology opens up a new world of Web3-enabled trade that is safer and more secure.. Investors can improve the value of their investment without having to sell by using the assets that support their tokens to cover expenses in the real world, diversify their holdings, or in other ways.

Smart DeFi puts some of blockchain technology's best features on show. Technology that is straightforward, usable, and creative is assisting in enhancing the industry's safety and inventiveness.

What is a FEG token:

According to FEG, the primary goal of its token is to offer a decentralized transaction network that runs on the BNB Chain and the Ethereum blockchain. The maximum circulating supply of the hyper-deflationary token FEG, which also features an inaccessible burn wallet, is 100 quadrillion on both chains above.

All holders, including the burn wallet, which serves as a holder and accumulates tokens throughout a transaction period, are subject to a 2% transaction tax that is dispersed based on the percentage of ownership. The developers want to emphasize that there is no burn limit. Doing so will allow customers to benefit from a "never-ending cycle of passive revenue with positive pricing pressure."

TikTok Holds the Key to Defi's Future

Despite the younger generation's lack of disposable income, short-form social media films have helped them become financially smart. TikTok reached 3 billion downloads in July 2021, and the social network claims to have more than 1 billion users that log on each month. Additionally, the platform is currently more well-liked among Generation Z in the US than Instagram.

From its all-time high north of $69,000 in 2021, Bitcoin (BTC $16,557) has decreased by more than 70% during the past six months. Market turbulence is anticipated, but if decentralized finance is to have a future, more people must accept it. Many investors are turned off by the volatility above and the skepticism around cryptocurrencies. Fortunately, investors in Generation Z are different from investors in other generations.

Digitally savvy and financially literate

The popularity of TikTok's monetary options has created a new portmanteau. Along with the social network, financial-related content, dubbed FinTok, has experienced a spectacular surge. The #Crypto hashtag received 1.9 billion videos last year as it went viral. Uploads using the hashtag #NFT rose by an astounding 93,000%. (further fueled by the general boom in NFT interest). Additionally, videos with the hashtag #StockTok received 1.4 billion views.

Money management videos are abundant outside of the crypto industry. More than 4.4 billion people viewed the content under the hashtag #PersonalFinance last year, which covered everything from tax and budgeting to savings and debt. It demonstrates that today's youth have a voracious thirst for financial information when taken into account in the context of TikTok's primary user base, Generation Z. They want to watch it while listening to catchy pop music and popular dance.

Young individuals are also leading the adoption of digital assets. CNBC's "Invest in You" study found that 18 to 34-year-olds invested 15% of all cryptocurrencies, compared to 11% for 35 to 64-year-olds and a pitiful 4% for 65 and above. The issue is that a sizeable portion of the 18–34 age group only views cryptocurrency as a 12-month strategy, according to 21% of 18–34-year-olds.

Unsurprisingly, Gen Z is learning about finance and embracing cryptocurrencies. The global investment returns yearbook published by Credit Suisse predicts that Gen Z will get a third lower return on traditional stock and bond investments than prior generations.

The COVID-19 epidemic has affected Generation Z's professional and financial prospects similarly to how the Great Recession affected millennials, according to Bank of America's "OK Zoomer" research report from December. Therefore, even though the majority of Generation Z needs more financial resources to invest in cryptocurrencies, they may do so in the future, particularly if they are as financially astute and motivated to make investments as the data indicates. That is where DeFi has a chance.

Transparent marketing is key to establishing trust in digital assets.

DeFi companies must engage the appropriate consumers in methods specifically catered to those demographics for the growth and health of the digital asset market.

Social media platforms like TikTok democratize the investment process, much like DeFi promises to do with finance. What was once a private community open only to certified hedge fund managers and Wall Street bankers is now open to everyone.

However, DeFi needs to improve its marketing if it wants to take advantage of the prospects offered by the most popular social media site. This entails producing short, to-the-point videos that are clear and concise, specific to the target audience, and that not only make cryptocurrency accessible but enjoyable while being open and honest about the risks associated with investing.

TikTok's short videos are popular but tend to focus on top-of-the-funnel activities. That could be a wonderful thing, but it could also be bad. Brands may engage Generation Z consumers today to prepare them to become informed leads ready to be converted when they have the money to invest in a few years.

This conversion-related content is required. Over the coming years, cryptocurrency companies must earn the audience's trust. This will be challenging, given the recent market volatility and negative attention the bear market has received.

DeFi companies must maintain their transparency, set themselves apart from TradFi businesses, and identify the types of video content that can foster enduring, dependable relationships with the younger generation. Bitcoin and other digital assets may have a bright future if crypto firms start speaking their language today.

Key features in this chapter

- DeFi will revolutionize banking and financial services in a similar way that artificial intelligence and machine learning in FinTech is upending the wealth management industry.
- Impacts of decentralized finance on competition, antitrust policy, and economic growth, decentralized finance, or the use of blockchain technology in financial services, can improve financial market efficiency, encourage competition, make it easier for small enterprises to acquire money, and stimulate economic development.
- Defi aims to make it possible for individual users to lend to, borrow from, manage assets from, or buy insurance directly from one another without using intermediaries.
- The potential presence of an "admin key" to the platform's code presents another risk to users of Defi systems.
- RegTech may provide a way to allow DeFi's financial gains, all while addressing user and financial regulator concerns and the significant problem that the rule of law in financial services presents for all parties, including developers, customers, and governments.
- In essence, embedded supervision is an automatic type of compliance.
- The EOEO also requests that the Federal Reserve chairman look into the possibility of a central bank digital currency (CBDC) using Defi architecture to improve payment system efficiency and reduce costs.

- The United States has to embrace the benefits offered by Defi, such as quick payments and custody of assets in digital form, as former SEC chairman Jay Clayton said in a column earlier this year (2022).
- To send a strong message, the DOJ should go after lawbreakers while the SEC issues guidelines for the safe keeping of tokenized assets.

Dear Reader,

As independent authors, it's often difficult to gather reviews compared with much bigger publishers.

Therefore, please leave a review on the platform where you bought this book.

KINDLE:

<u>LEAVE A REVIEW HERE</u> < click here >

Many thanks,

Author Team

CONCLUSION

A new financial system called decentralized finance allows users to send and receive money from any other user with only an internet connection and a digital wallet. DeFi does away with the usage fees banks and other financial institutions impose by eliminating intermediaries. Peer-to-peer interactions are made possible by smart contracts. Decentralized financial institutions (DeFi) allow users to conduct transactions without involving a middleman. Accounts post only numerical addresses and are thus pseudo-anonymous.

Peer-to-peer lending can satisfy a person's desire for a loan. DeFi developers have unlocked numerous new asset-decentralized finance potentials by implementing immutable smart contracts on the blockchain.

Furthermore, DeFi lending entails providing cryptocurrency loans through a decentralized network. These loans enable cryptocurrency owners to lend their assets and earn high-interest rates. Compared to the rates provided by conventional banks, these interest rates are more profitable..

With the sudden collapse of FTX, it has driven investors into self-custody and decentralized finance platforms. Almost 97% of all cryptocurrency stolen in the first quarter of 2022 has been taken from DeFi protocols. Delegates are reminded of their responsibility and are moving toward DEXs and DeFi platforms. It is now a past memory that the cryptocurrency market had reached record highs in 2021 before collapsing in 2022. Leading crypto lenders and exchanges also failed when the market value fell.

Despite this event, decentralized finance has shown an impressive adoption curve. Authorities will be careful to strike a balance between regulatory control and innovation as the DeFi program allows financial institutions to take custody of and actively manage digital assets for third parties.

As the total supply of DeFi tokens rises, the value of existing tokens is diminished by the creation of LPT or lending tokens. Financial institutions are well-suited to map new regulations since they already have to adhere to various regulations in their core business. Lack of consumer protection and unstable markets will always threaten the adoption of DeFi.

Currently, assets worth nearly $70 million are locked in DeFi protocols worldwide. FightOut is an in-app, off-chain digital fitness project and Dash 2 Trade project is scheduled to launch its initial exchange offering (IEO) on January 23. MKR could also be the greatest Defi cryptocurrency to purchase this year.

The year, 2022, was challenging for the DeFi and crypto industries. Scams, and hacking, have severely damaged the trust in the sector. The use of blockchain increased across all industries, but regulation is inevitable. There are only 100 million DeFi tokens in circulation, and none more may be produced. The DeFi industry has grown by 47% over the past year and according to our DEFC price projection, the coin may cost $0.95 by the end of 2023.

Looking ahead, 2023 is surely anticipated to be a significant year for blockchain, cryptocurrencies, and DeFi.

Made in United States
Orlando, FL
27 March 2024

45174673R00129